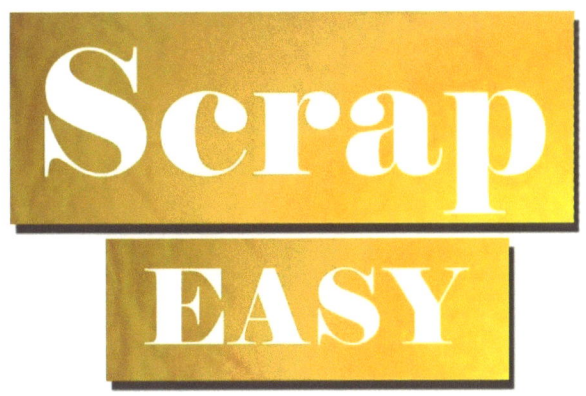

BUILDING A COLLAGE QUILT

Aisha Lumumba

ISBN:
ISBN-13: 978-0-991130511
ISBN-10: 0991130510

DEDICATION

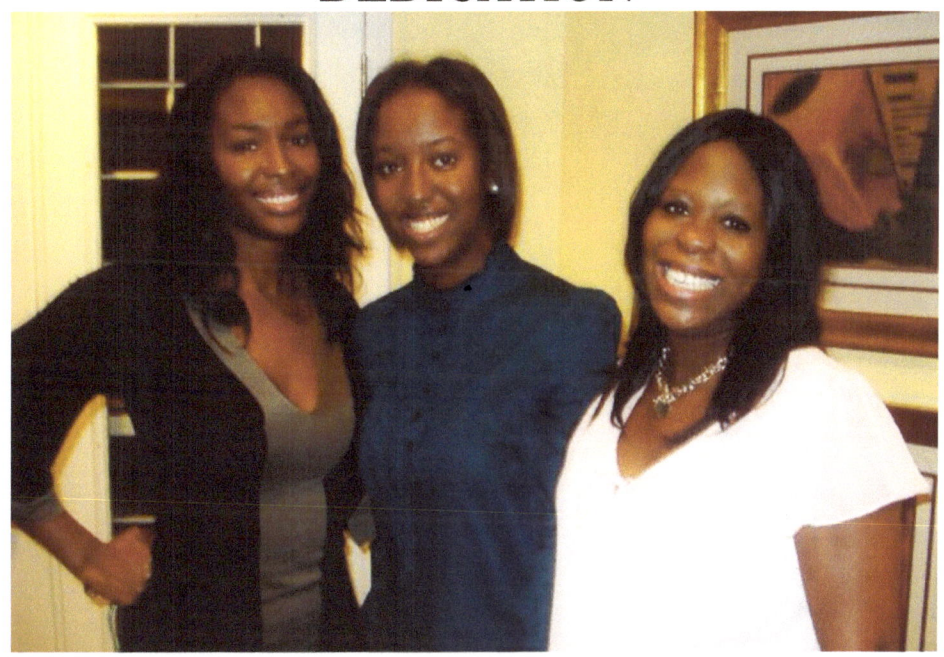

This book is dedicated to my beautiful daughters: Malaika Lumumba, Sharifa Lumumba and Anane Lumumba. The "Hair Revolution" continues.

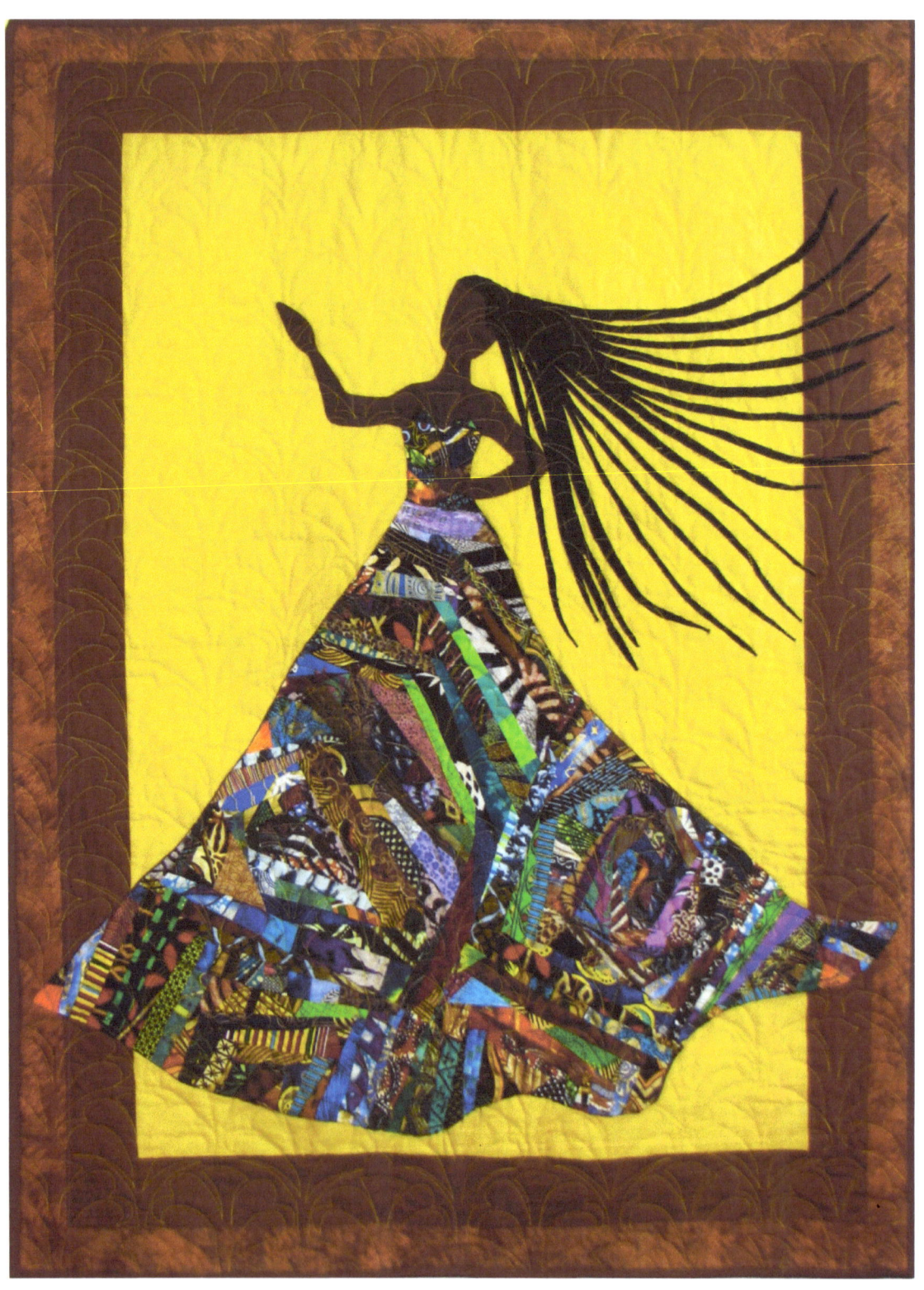

CONTENTS

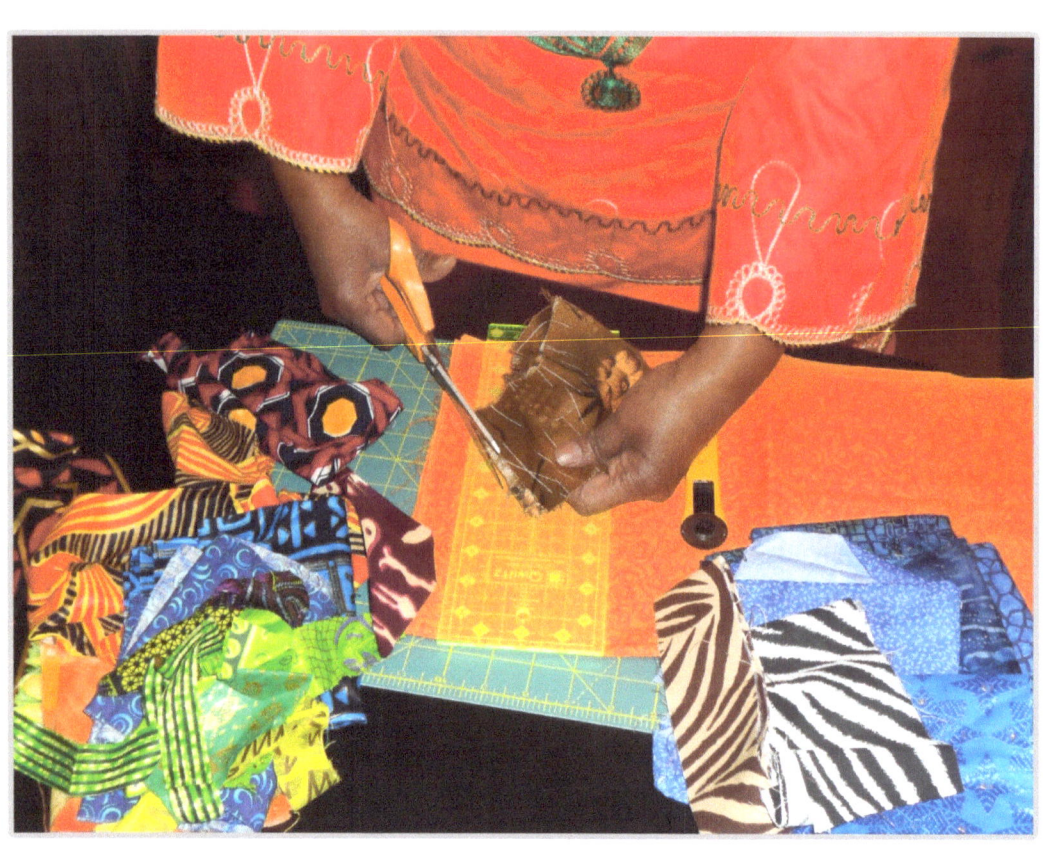

INTRODUCTION

I started quilting because I had so many boxes of scrap fabric left over from my many projects. My love affair with fabric probably began when my mother held me in that first baby blanket. It continued with soft bedding and cute dresses. Then I started to sew clothes. I made all my own outfits and slowly ventured out to make clothes for others. I saved every little scrap in an attempt to be frugal. We had very little of everything, so salvaging was big in our household.

Whenever I work, I save any scrap that can be cut in a two inch square. In the past my thought was that someday I would make quilts from all my scraps. I had boxes and boxes of scraps. When my husband threatened to throw the boxes away, I started quilting.

I had one little scrap of fabric that was too small to use in any quilt pattern I had, but I loved it too much to throw it away. I moved it around, put it away, pulled it out again, put it away. One day I sewed another piece of fabric to it and then another to that. I kept adding until I had about an eight inch square. I built the block using the same technique as the log cabin pattern. It became the beginning of my first scrappy quilt. I must admit that working with small scraps is time consuming, but oh so rewarding. The freedom of this "build and trim" system enhances creativity.

I'd also be remiss if I let you think that the choice of colors and fabrics was completely random. I tried putting some scraps in a bag once. I stuck my hand in the bag and sewed whatever came out. It was a disaster. I am much too controlling to do it that way. I saw a woman teaching a class on doing it randomly. She was smart enough to put light colors in one bag and dark colors in another. Then she alternated them. I am sure that would have worked better for me, but I really like to see what I am putting together before hand. I do a kind of mix between random and control. I pick two pieces, stand back to see how it feels to me. If it feels right, I keep it. If it clashes, I change it. If it is leaning towards one color too much, I change it. It's like deciding which shoes to wear with an outfit.

Welcome to creativity and freedom with fabrics. I now give you the freedom to put it all together any way you wish. You can be as conservative or as daring as you want.

.

CHAPTER ONE
SUPPLIES NEEDED

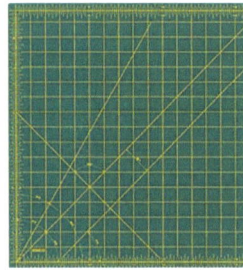 **Cutting Mat**

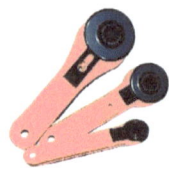 **Rotary Cutter**

 **Thread:** neutral color (like black, gray or white) for general piecing.

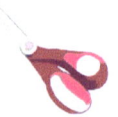 **Scissors**

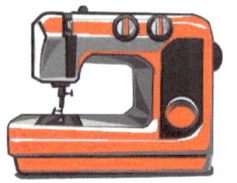 **Sewing Machine**

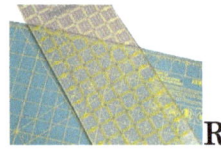 **Ruler**

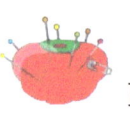 **Pins**

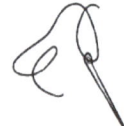 **Hand Sewing Needles**

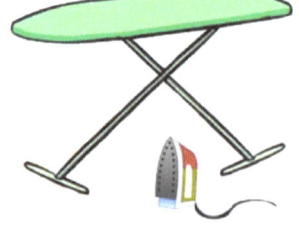 **Iron and Board**

Fabrics Needed:

Background fabric	one yard
Border #1	half (½) yard
Border #2	half (½) yard
Binding	half (½) yard*
Head and body	half (½) yard
Hair	three-fourths (3/4) yard
Dress	scraps/or one and half (1½)yard
Batting	crib size 40"x 60"
Backing	two yards

*(I generally use the same fabric for Border #2 and binding. So I buy one yard of same color).

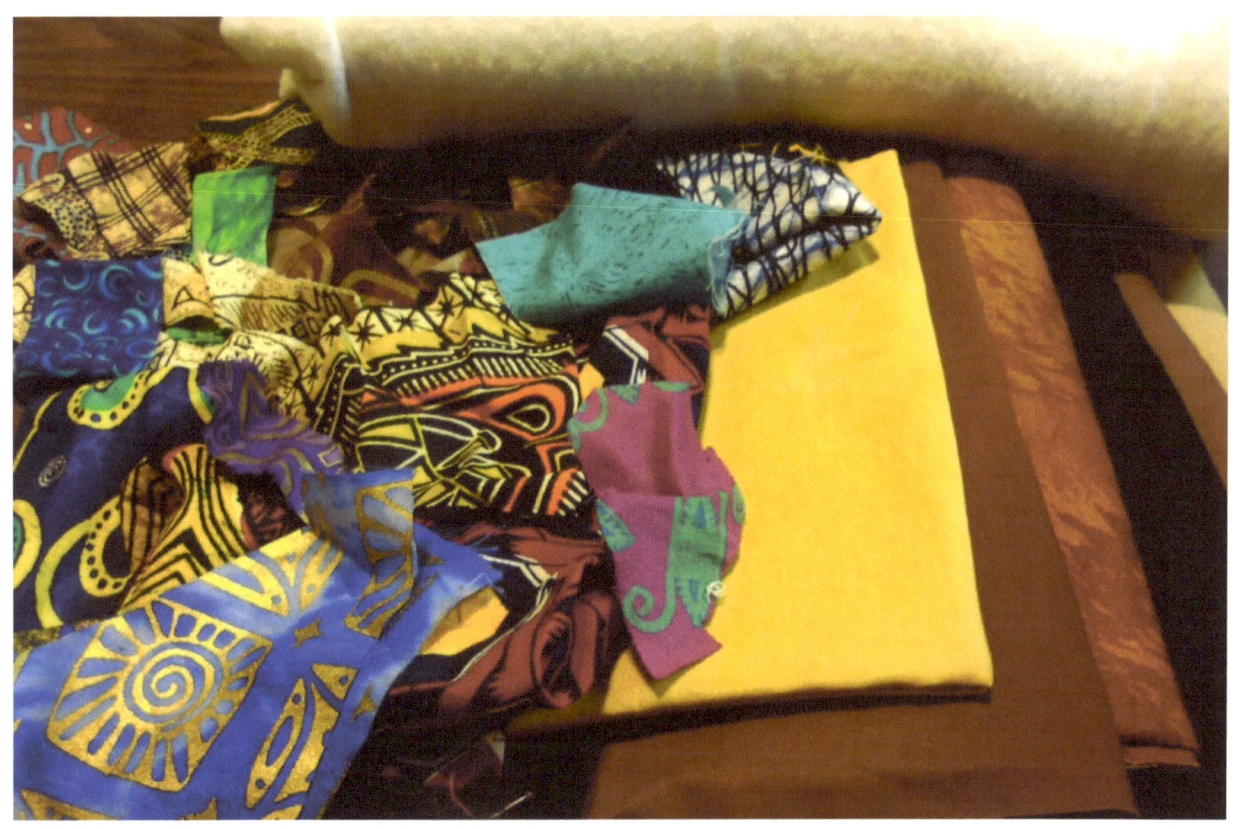

CHAPTER TWO
BUILDING THE BLOCK

The blocks are built on the idea of the log cabin crazy quilt pattern, but does not follow the rigid design. It is acceptable to go from left to right and then change around and add in the opposite direction. There are literally no rules. Keeping strips a similar size seems to work well, for instance if the center is about 1" at the widest point, then 1" width is the approximate standard (but not rigid) for the rest of the pieces.

I use a lot of different color prints. Sometimes I have enough scraps in my bag to repeat a print and sometimes I don't. Repetition ties the blocks together visually. I use a sew and trim system. I trim them with various angles to keep it interesting.

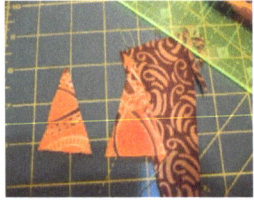

1. Start with one small scrap any shape. Add another small scrap to it as soon in figure. This will be the beginning of your block

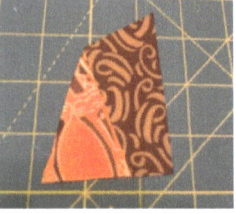

2. Press and then trim. Be creative with shape. No rules.

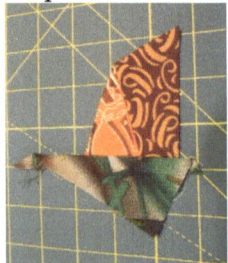

3. Add another scrap and press.

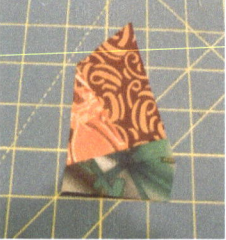

4. Trim in random shape.

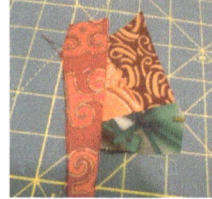

5. Add another scrap. Random color.

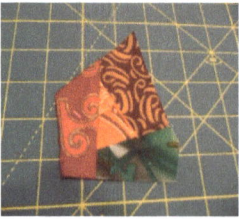

6. Trim while keeping the idea of random shapes. Add strips clockwise.

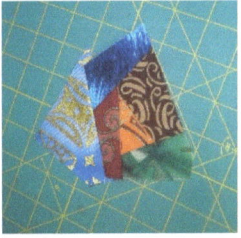

7. Continue to add scraps. Two blue print scraps have been added and trimmed.

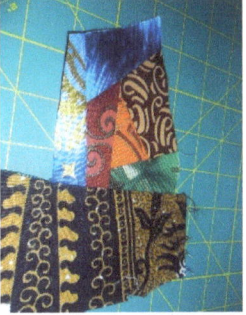

8. Add another scrap.

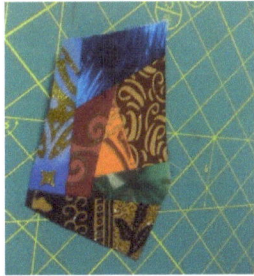

9. Trim in random shape.

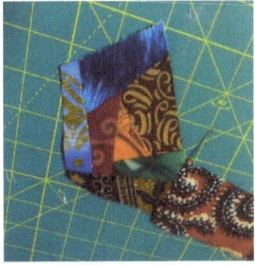

10. Add another scrap and trim.

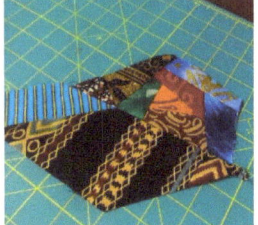

11. When the block starts to get larger I sew small scraps together to make a strip and add.

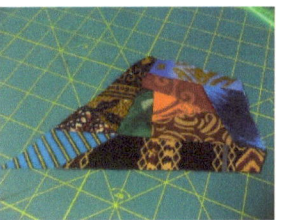

12. Trim in random shape.

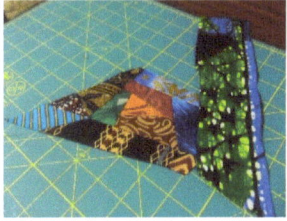

13 Add another scrap. Here I repeated the green color.

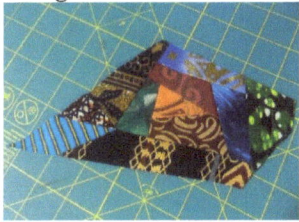

14. Trim in random shape.

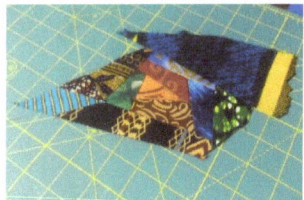

15. Add another scrap. Picked up more blue

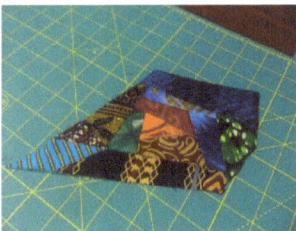

16. Trim in random shape.

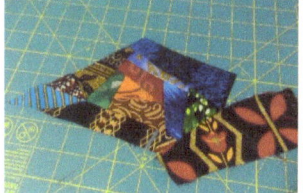

17. Add another scrap. Press

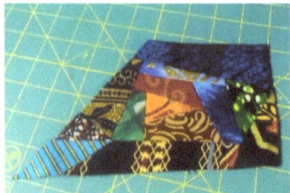

18. Trim

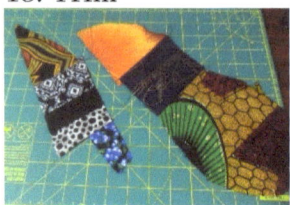

19. Sew scraps together into a strip.

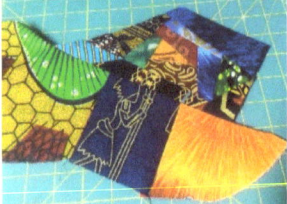

20. Add strip to block.

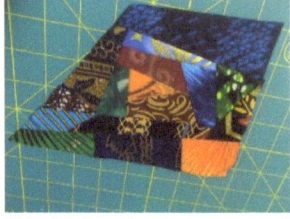

21. Trim in random shape.

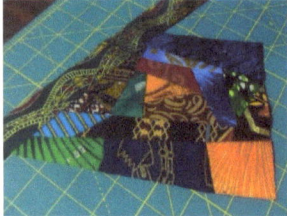

22. Add another scrap.

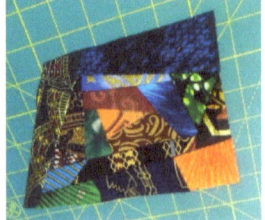

23. Trim in random shape.

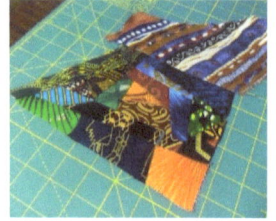

24. Add another scrap.

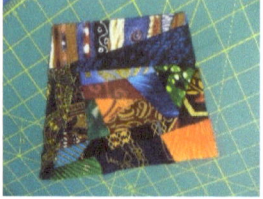

25. Trim.

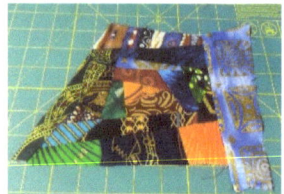

26. Add another scrap.

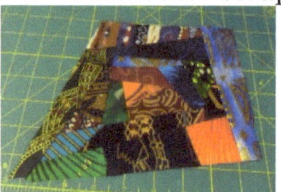

27. Trim in random shape.

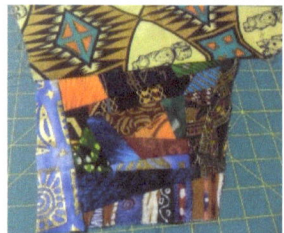

28. Add another scrap.

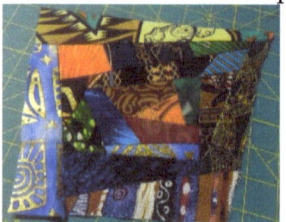

29. Trim.

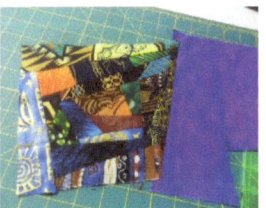

30. Add another scrap.

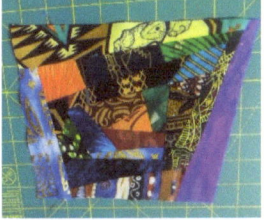

31. Trim in random shape.

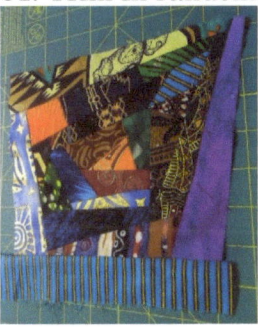

32. Add another scrap. At this point I start to gradually square up the block.

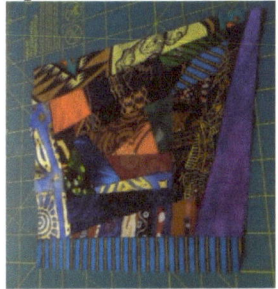

33. Press and trim.

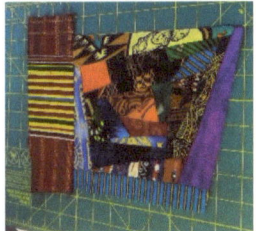

34. Add another scrap.

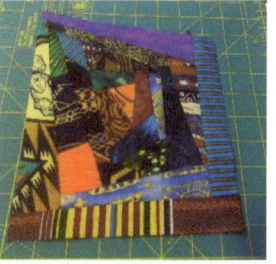

35. Trim in random shape.

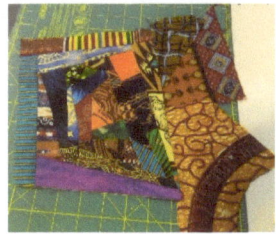

36. Add another scrap.

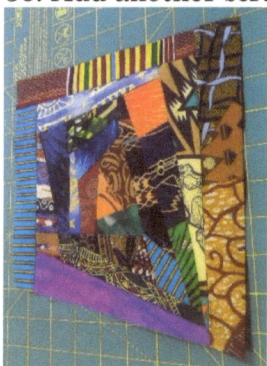

37. Trim in random shape.

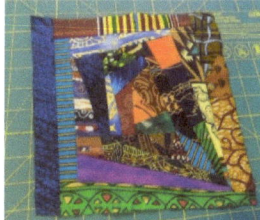

38. Continue to add and trim scraps. Here we added a green, a purple and black / red strip.

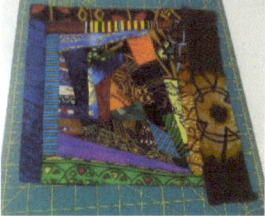

39 Add another scrap.

40. Trim

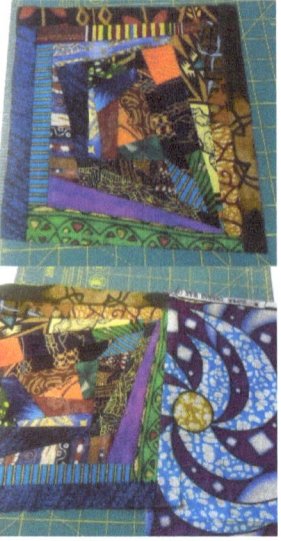

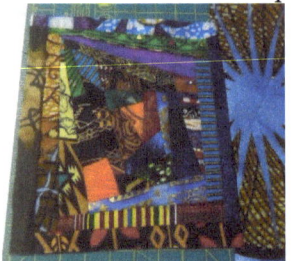

41. Add another scrap.

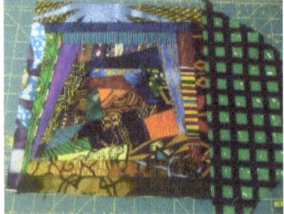

42. Continue adding strips and trimming in random shapes.

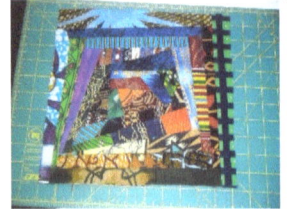

43. Add another scrap.

44. Trim in random shape.

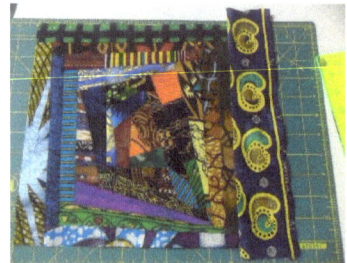

45. Add another scrap.

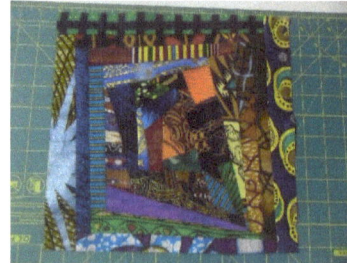

46. Trim to square.

Use this general procedure to make all the blocks.

CHAPTER THREE
BLOCKS

Make five or six blocks. Sometimes a block will be larger than the original 11" X 11" ideal. I keep working until it can be squared. Block three and Block six are examples of blocks that kept getting larger and larger. Although I made six blocks, I only used five because that one oversized (#three) block was almost the size of two blocks. I also could have cut it down but I liked the look of it.

Block #one

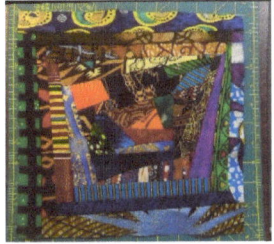

Block #four

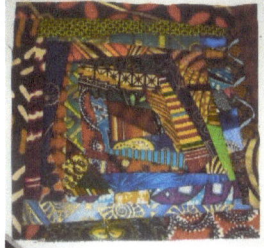

Block #two

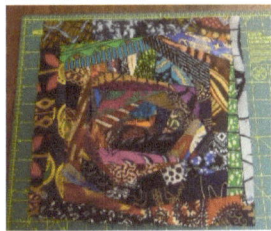

Block #five

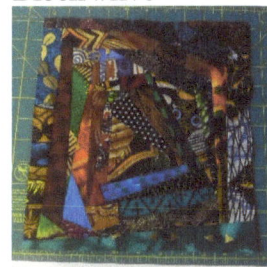

Block #three

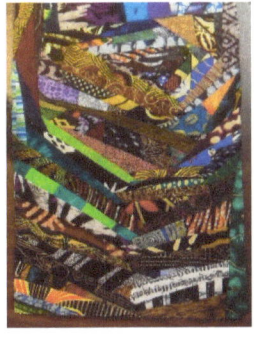

Block #six

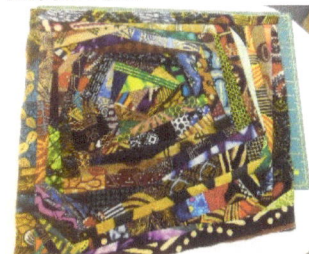

CHAPTER FOUR
BACKGROUND

One yard fabric for center background. Open yardage and press flat. Trim to approximate 30" x 42".

First border –Half yard for border. Cut four 3" strips. Sew to outside edges as shown below.

Second border -One yard for border and binding. Cut eight 2 ½" strips. Sew to outside edges as shown below. Set four aside for binding. Trim away selvage edge when cutting.

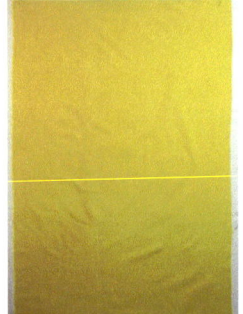
Background fabric

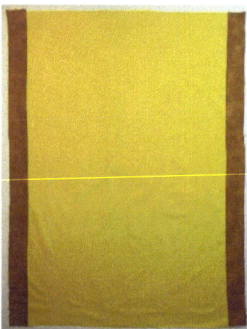
First border. Sew to both sides.

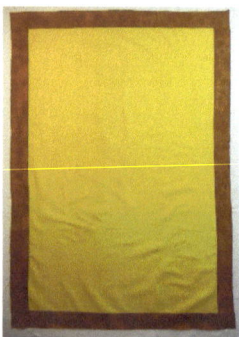
Sew to top and bottom

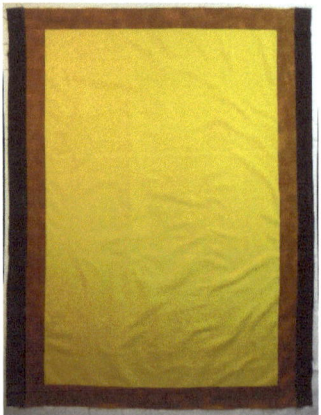

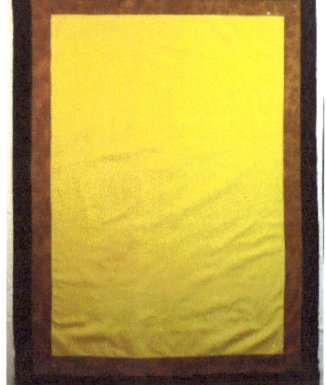

Add a second border to background.

CHAPTER FIVE
HEAD AND BODY

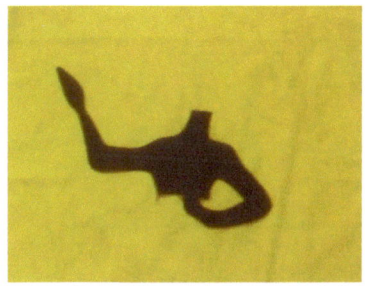

1. Cut two of body patterns. Line the body pattern by placing right sides facing each other. Sew around the side edges of pattern leaving the top (neck) and bottom (waist) open. Turn and press.

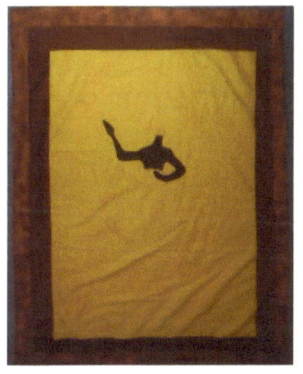

2. Place body about 14 inches from top of background.

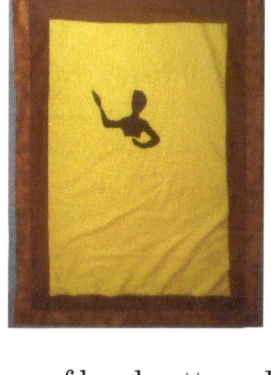

3. Cut two of head pattern. Line the head pattern by placing right sides facing each other. Sew all the way around the complete circle. Slit open in the lining and turn inside out. Press. Place head on body. Tilt back.

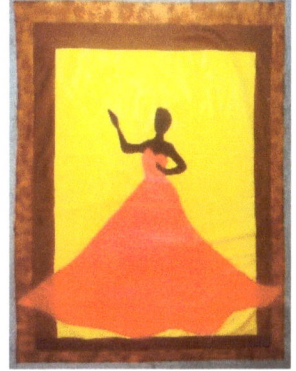

4. Use the pattern to adjust positioning of head and body.

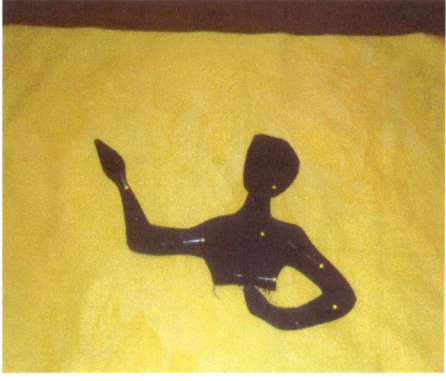

5. Pin body and head to background. Sew to background.

CHAPTER SIX
DRESS

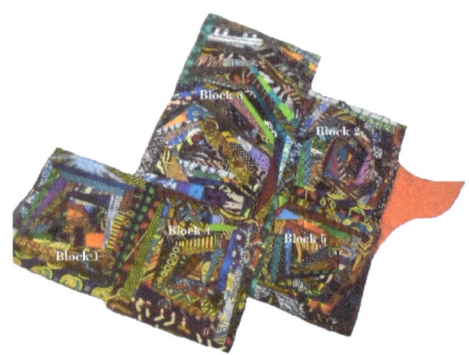

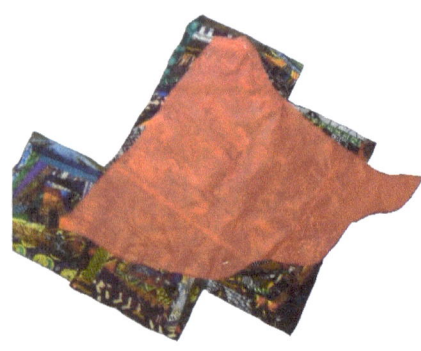

1. Place five blocks side by side on top of skirt pattern covering pattern as much as possible. *Note that one edge is not covered. Sew blocks together once design has been established.

2. Place skirt pattern on top of sewn blocks.

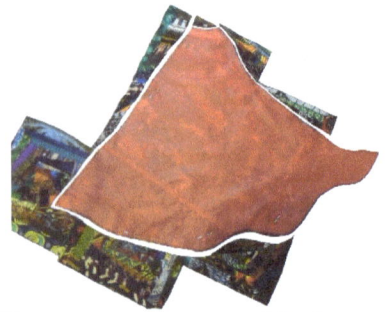

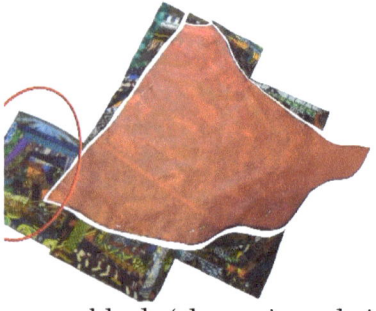

3. Pin pattern to sewn blocks and cut.

4. Take excess block (shown in red circle) and place on other side.

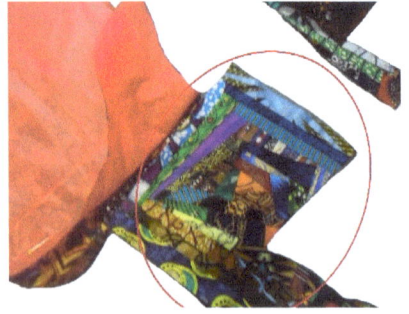

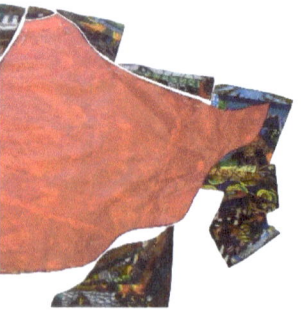

5. Sew left over to sewn blocks.

6. Pin pattern to new addition.

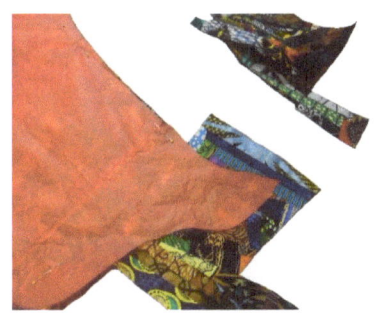

7. Cut remainder of pattern.

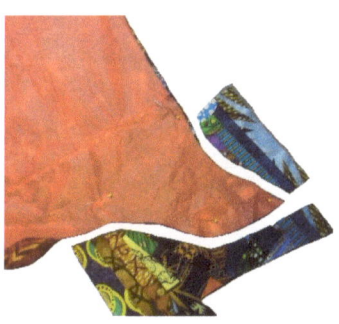

8. Save excess to cut bodice top.

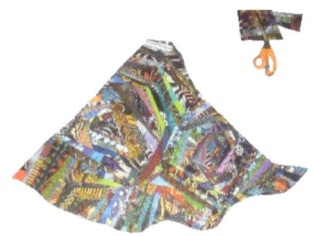

9. All done!

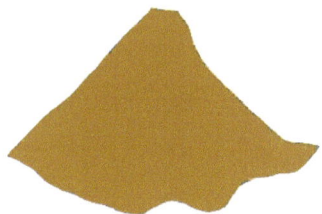

10. Cut lining and place on skirt with right sides facing. Sew all the way around the edges leaving the top (waist) open. Turn and iron.

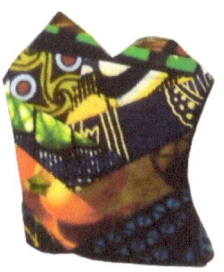

11. Cut bodice from left-over block. Line by sewing all the way around outside edges.

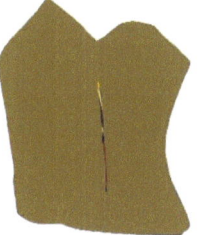

12. Slit lining in center and turn inside out. Iron flat

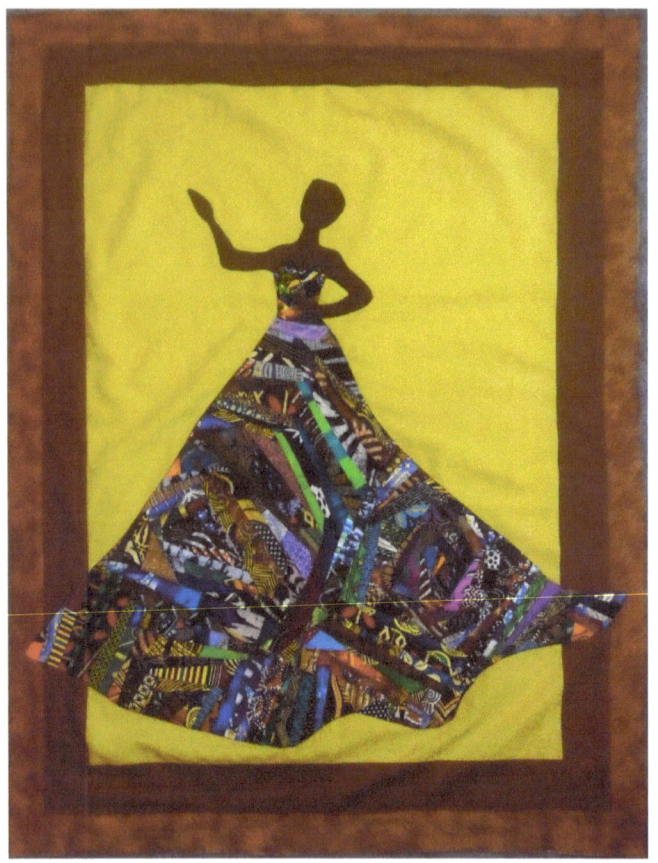

13. Place bodice top and skirt onto background. Appliqué pieces to background by hand or machine. (I prefer hand appliqué.)

Note: You may also skip lining each piece and sew directly to background as a raw edge appliqué.

CHAPTER SEVEN
HAIR

The hair is the most exciting part of this quilt. This quilt enhances the conversation about hair. I freely add pieces to the head as I wish. There are definitely no rules for the direction or length of the hair. This is the place where creativity can burst forth and make a hair statement. Make it long, make it short, tie it up, curl it, color it, do the same thing we do to our real hair; or simply make curvy strips and attach to the head as shown in photographs below. Use interfacing under the background when sewing the strips on.

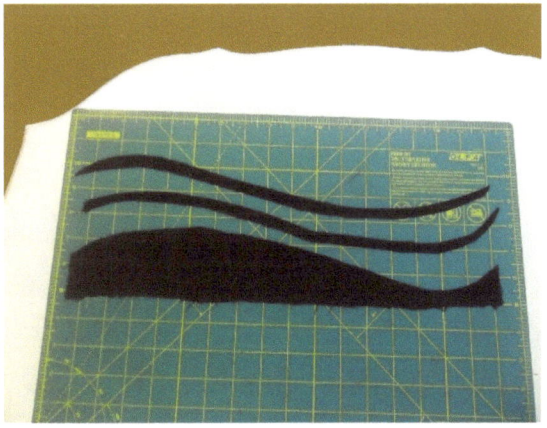

It takes about 20 to 25 strips to fill the head.

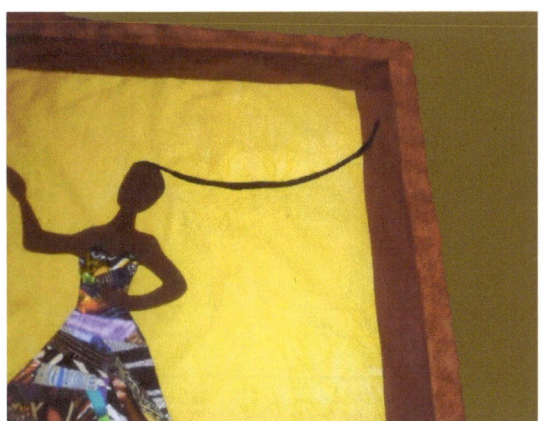
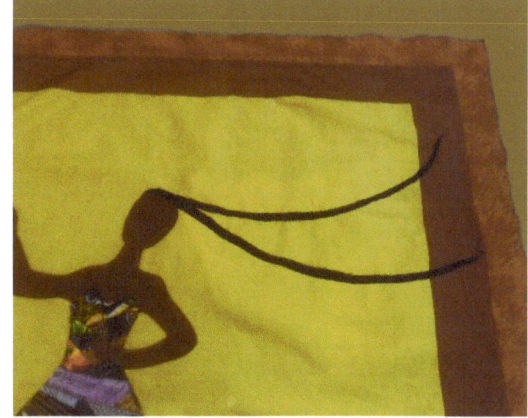

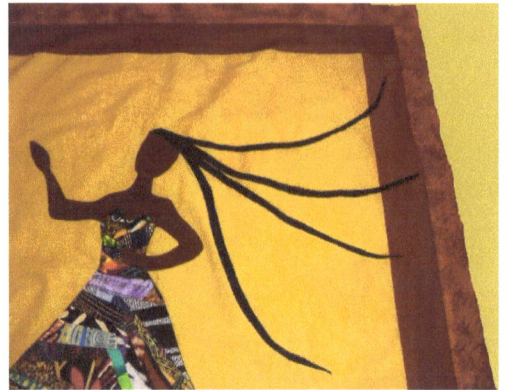

Start by placing four pieces.

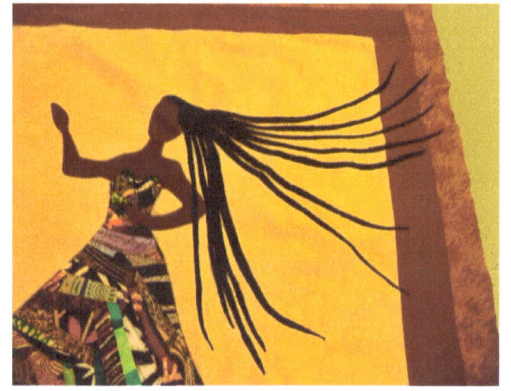

Fill in with strips.

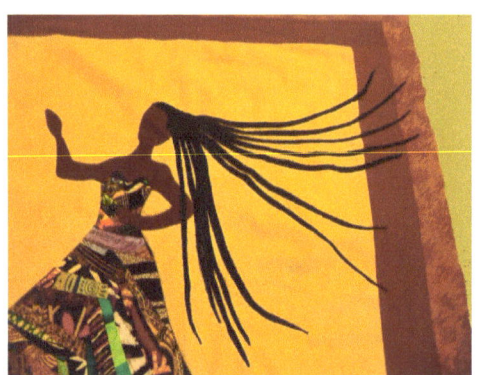

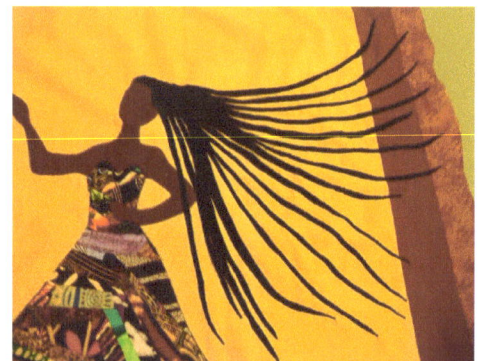

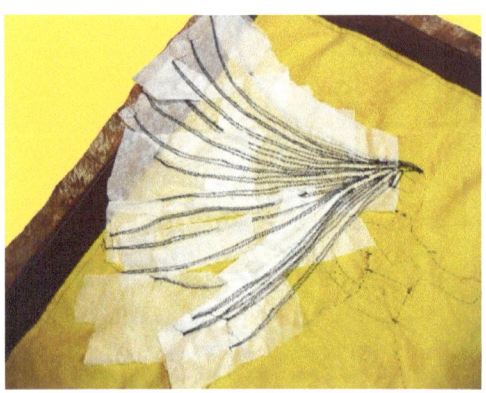

I use scraps of interfacing in keeping with the re-cycling re-using tradition. I don't always have scraps but like to use them when I can.

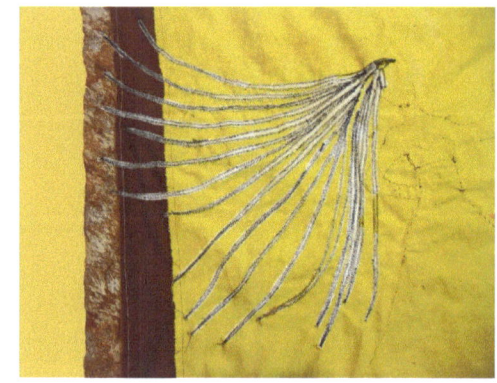

Trim excess interfacing away.

CHAPTER EIGHT
GALLERY

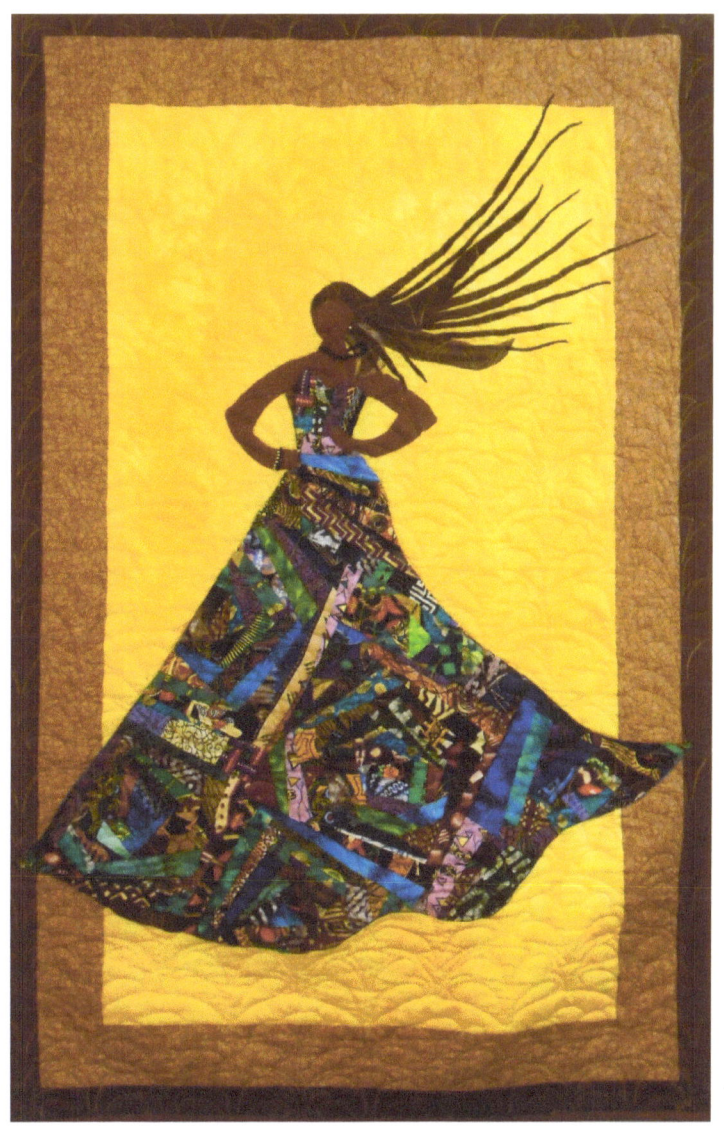

"I Am Not My Hair"
34" x 54"
2013

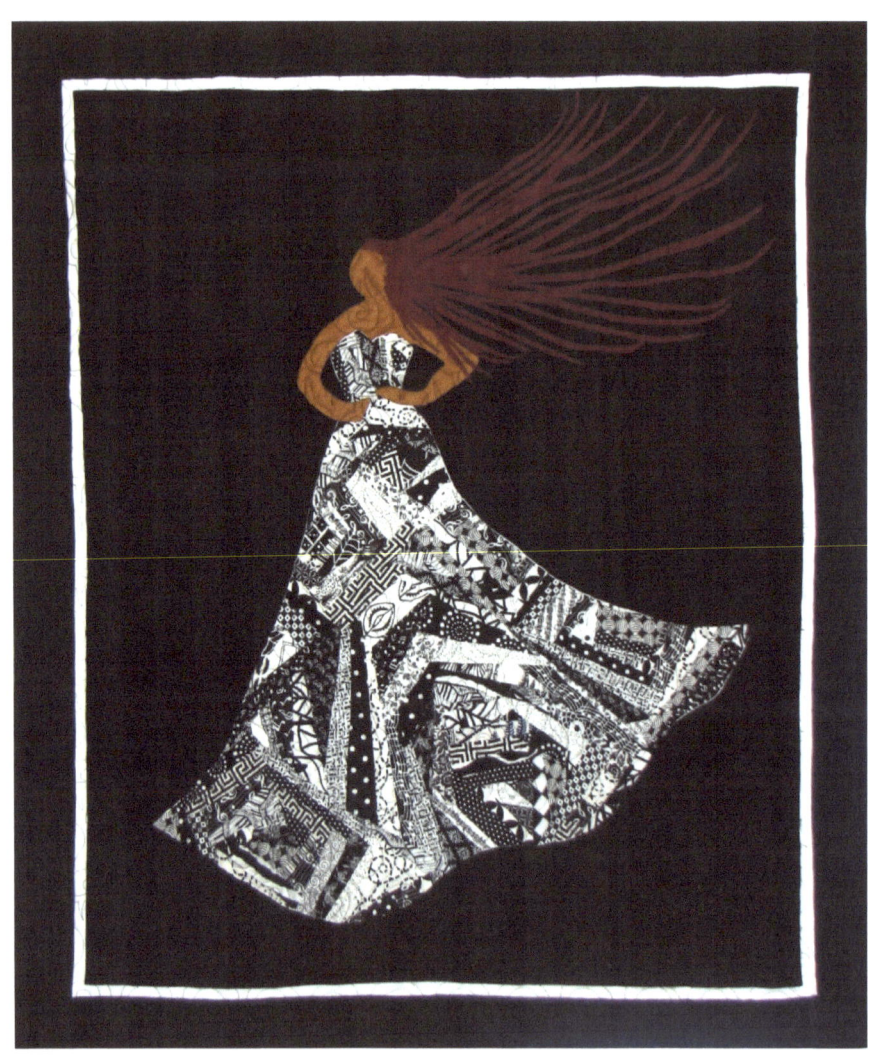

"I Am Not My Hair #2"
45" x 51"
2013

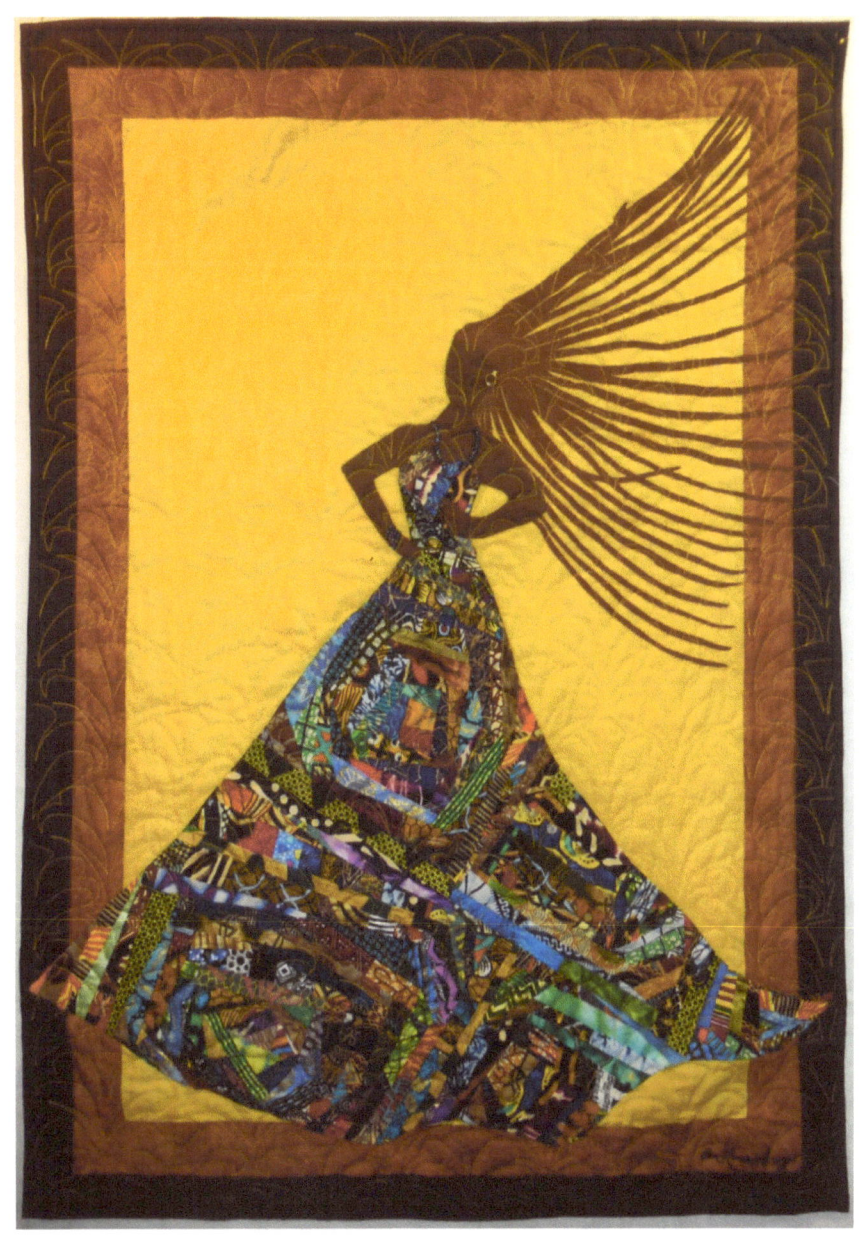

"I Am Not My Hair #3"
38" x 52"
2014

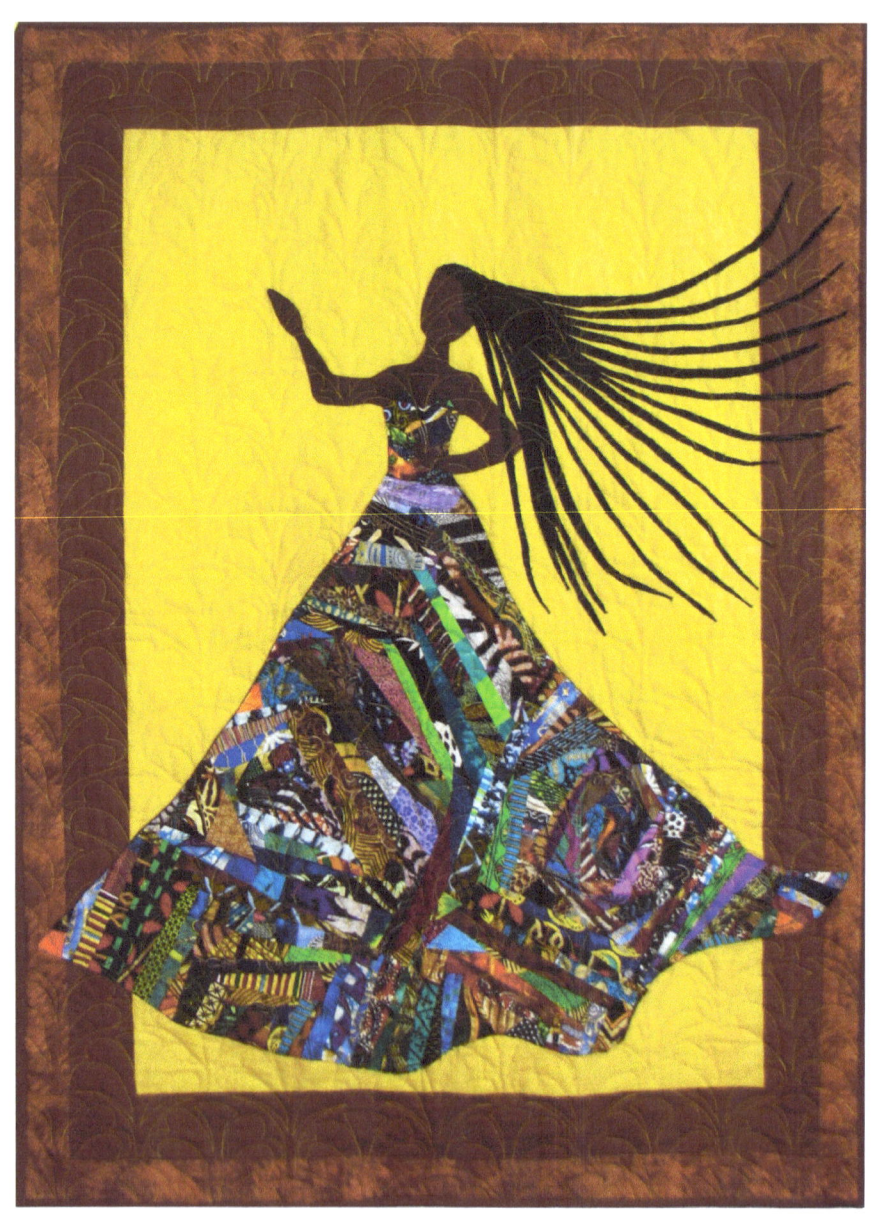

"Hair Revolution #1"
38" x 51"
2014

CHAPTER NINE
PATTERN

Piecing lady directions below.

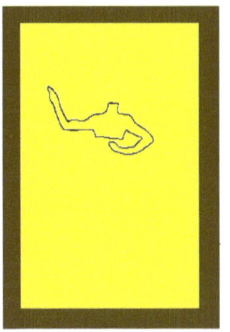 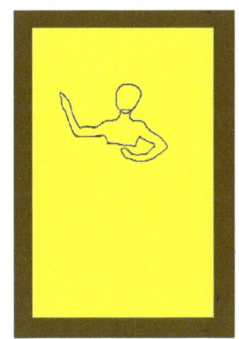 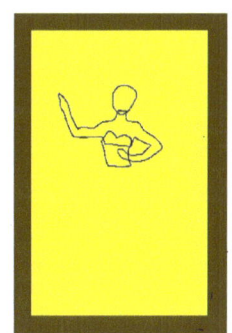

1. Attach body to the background fabric   2. Attach head to the neck onto background
3. Attach bodice to body   4. Attach skirt to bodice

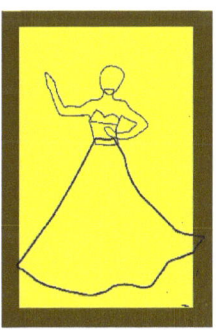 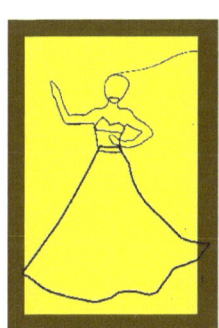 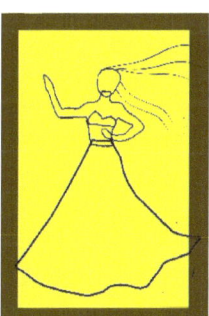

5,6, and so on. Attach strips for hair

The pattern on following pages can be enlarged to 435% at a copy center that has a Large Format Printer. It is usually a self-service feature.

I use an [Old School] Overhead Classroom Projector that I project the image onto the wall for enlargement.

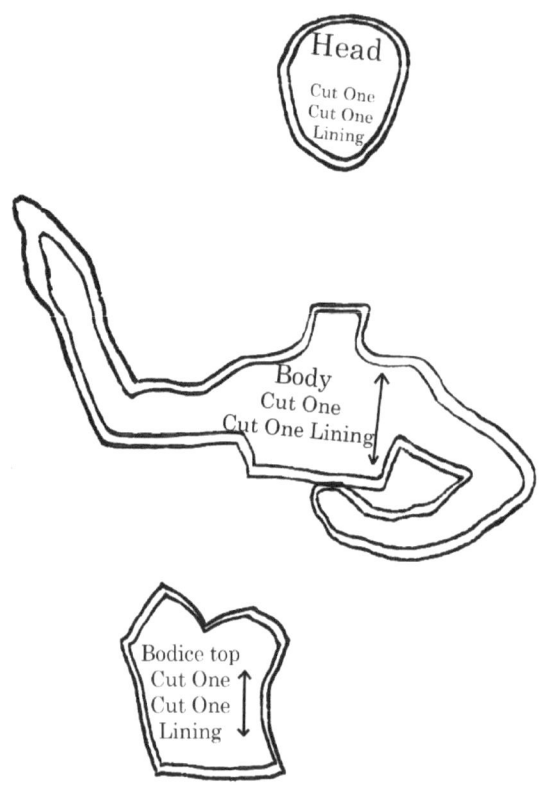

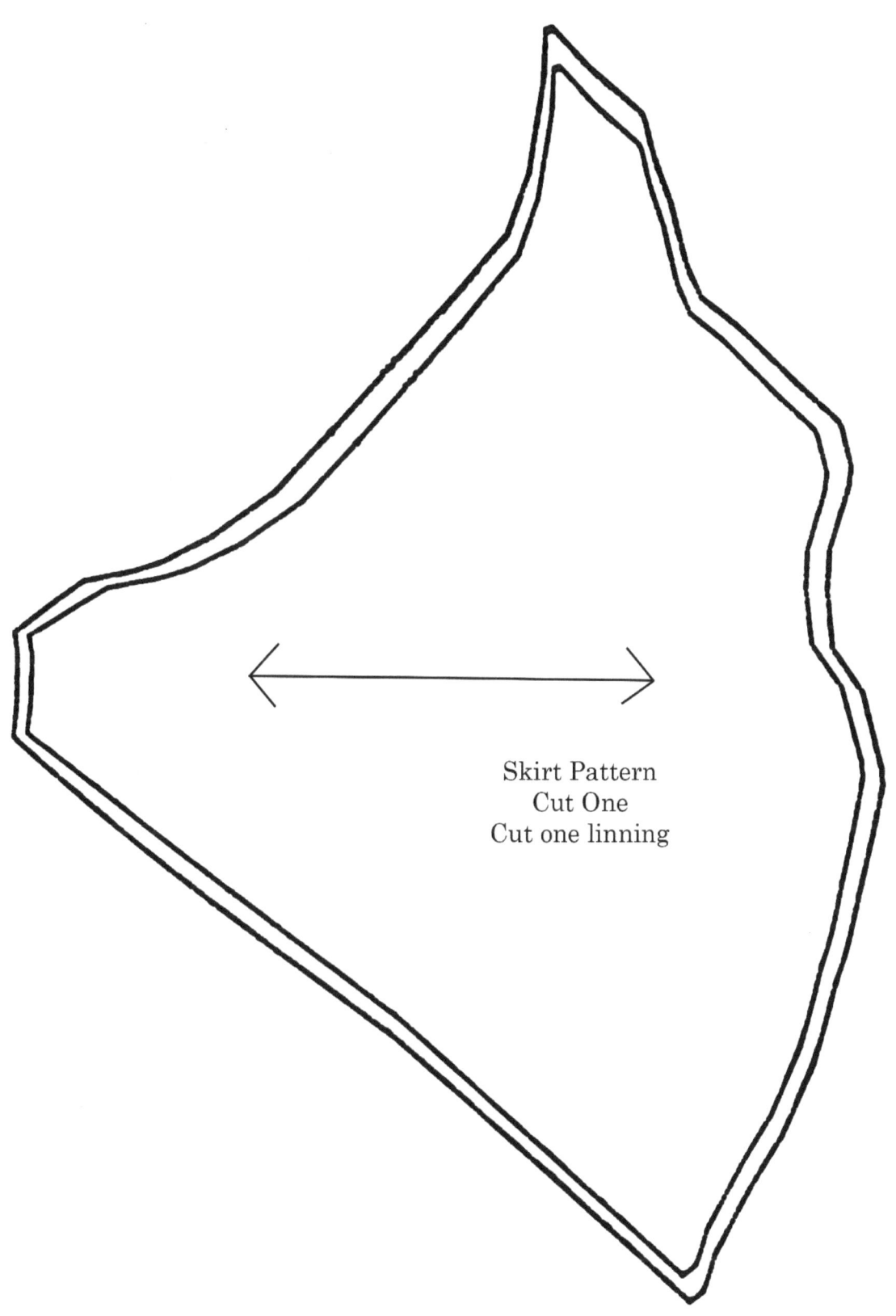

Skirt Pattern
Cut One
Cut one linning

CHAPTER TEN
PRINTER PATTERN

**Print the following pages to create actual size patterns.
Pages of Body and Skirt pattern need to be attached (tape or glue).**

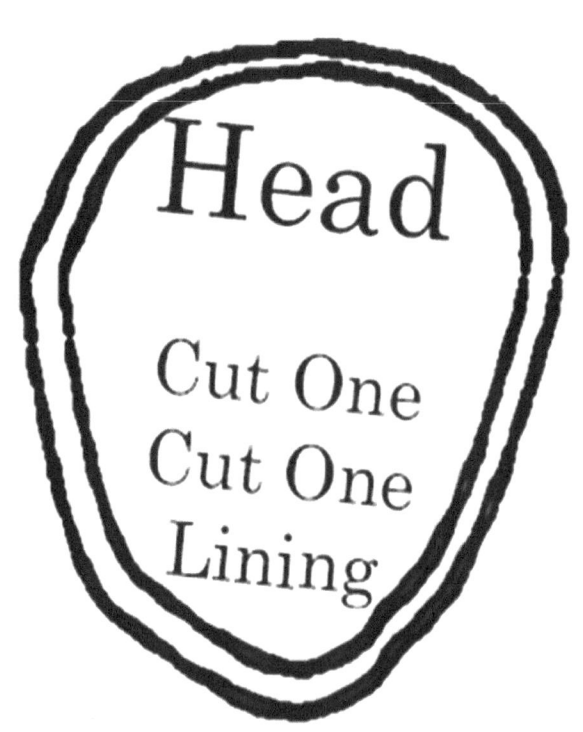

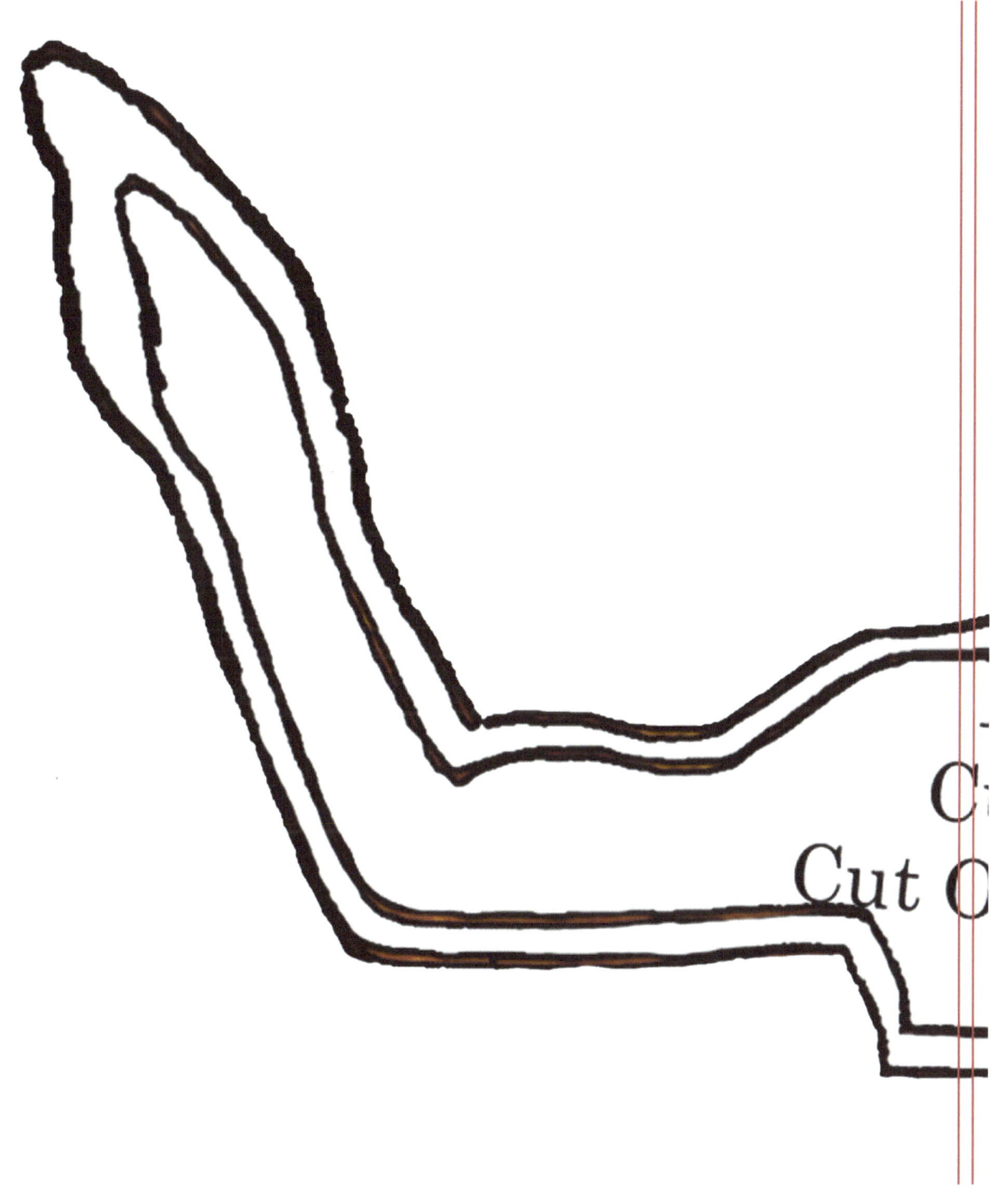

Cut O

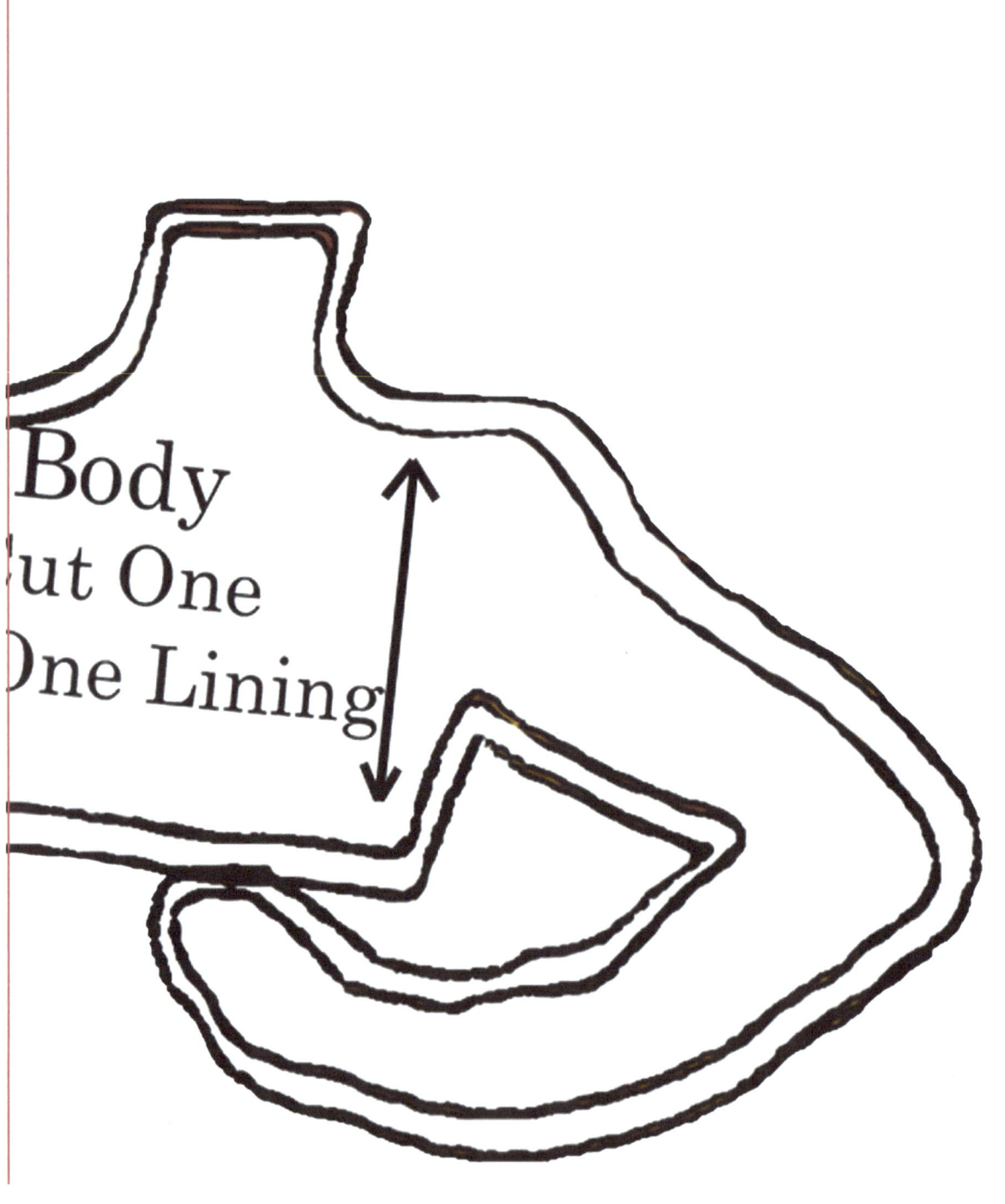

Body
Cut One
One Lining

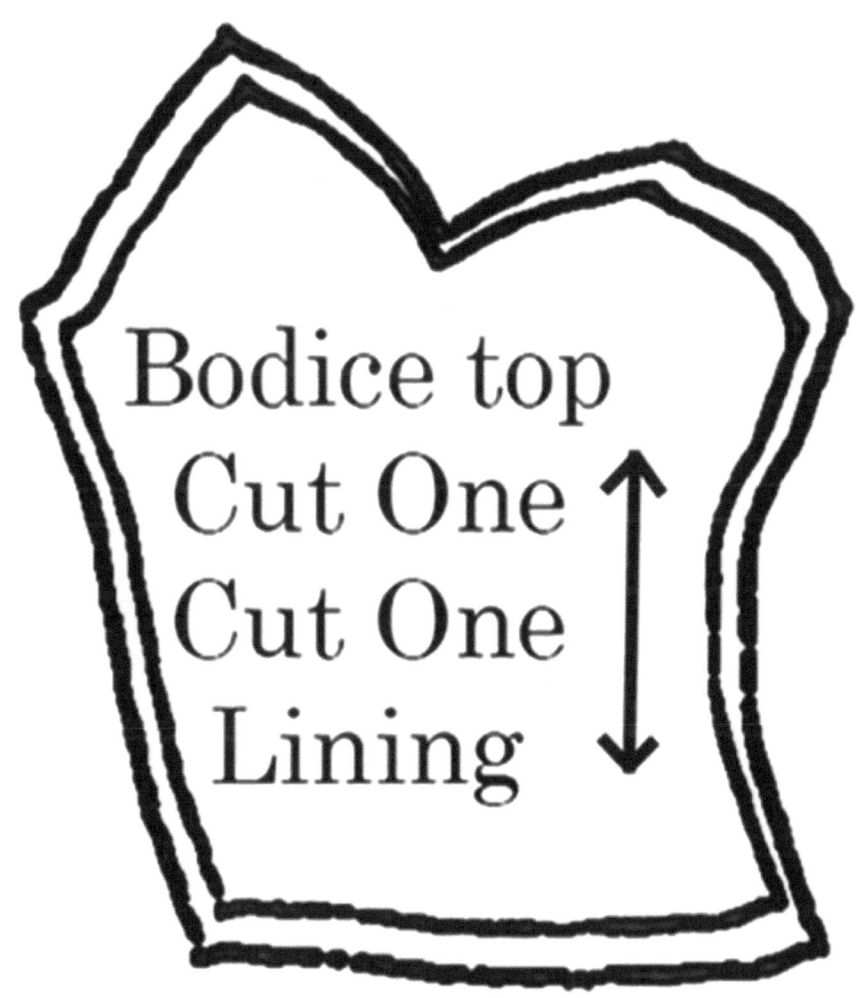

Skirt is a 15 page printable pattern. Page 1, Page 5, and Page 8 are completely blank. I have not added them here because you may simply use a blank sheet of paper to help with placement. Section overlaps on each sheet. Assemble as follows:

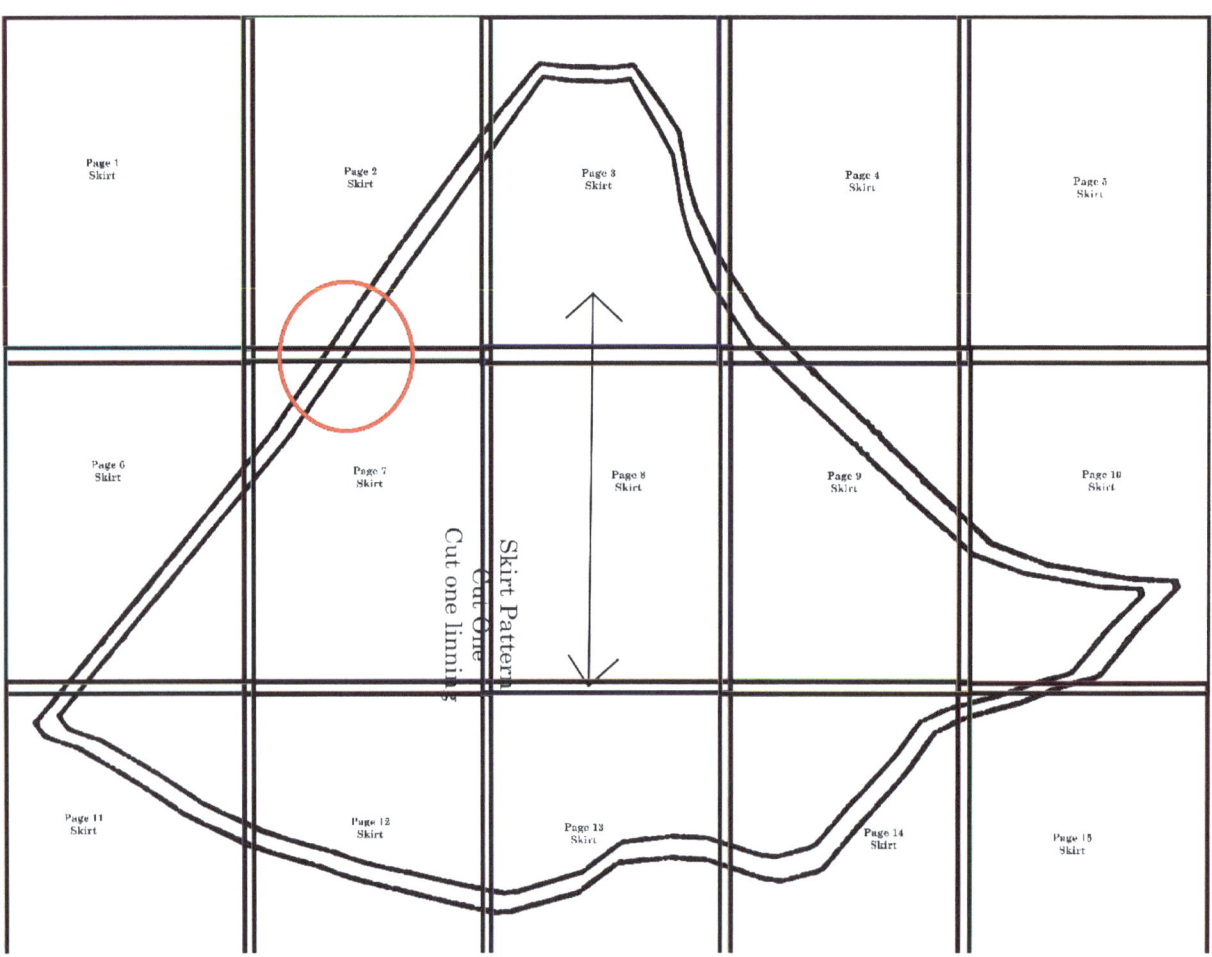

Page 2
Skirt

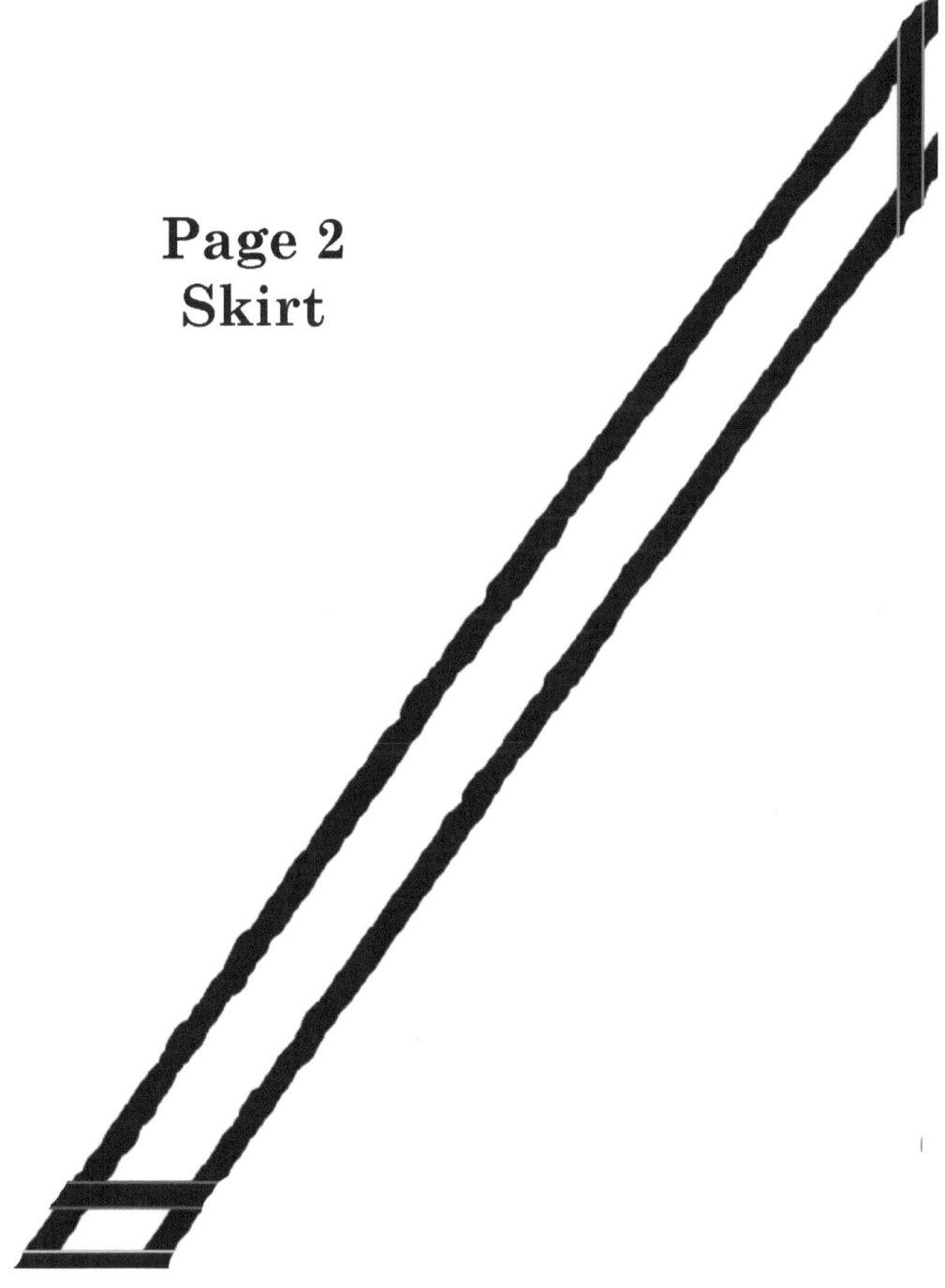

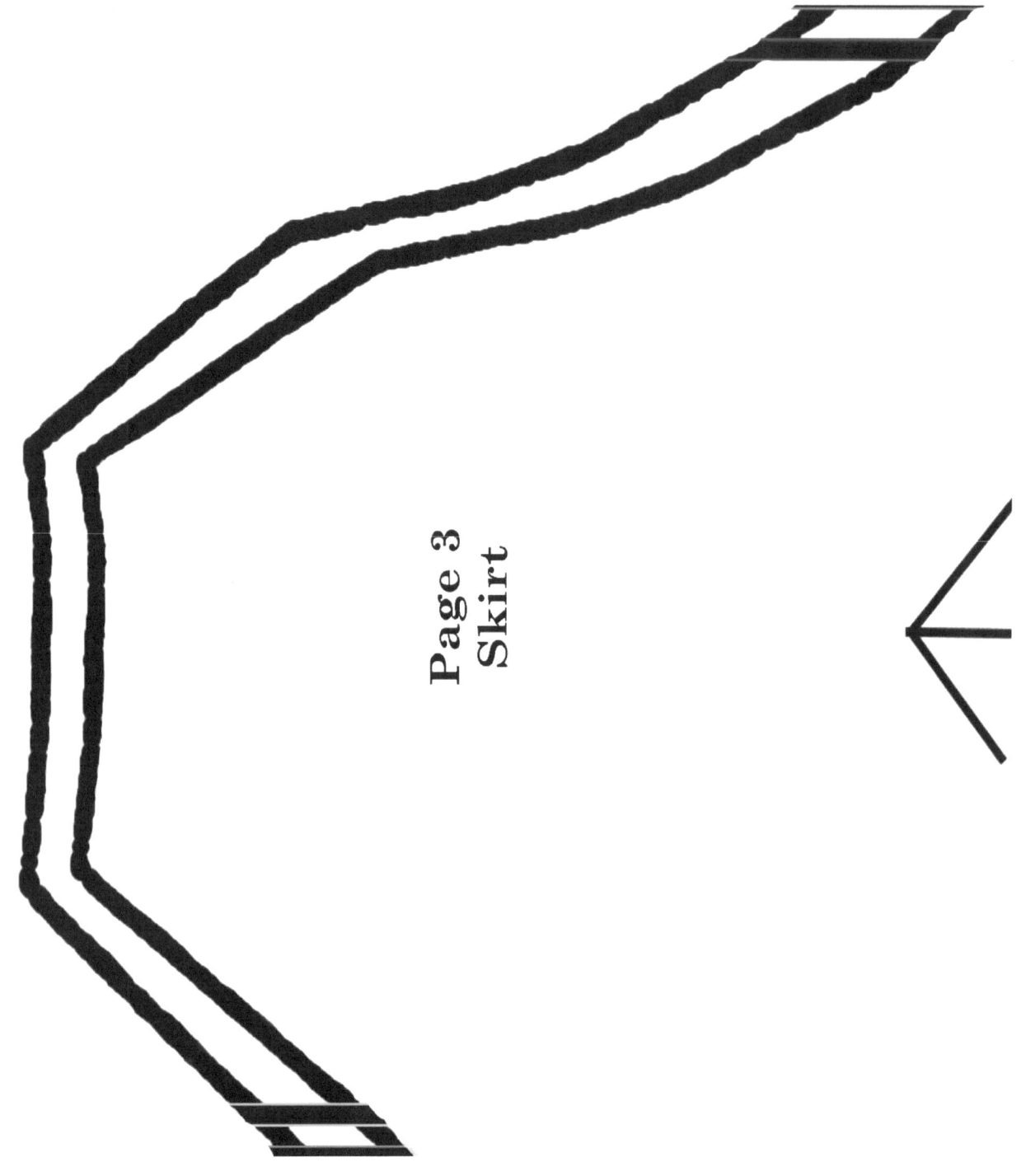

**Page 3
Skirt**

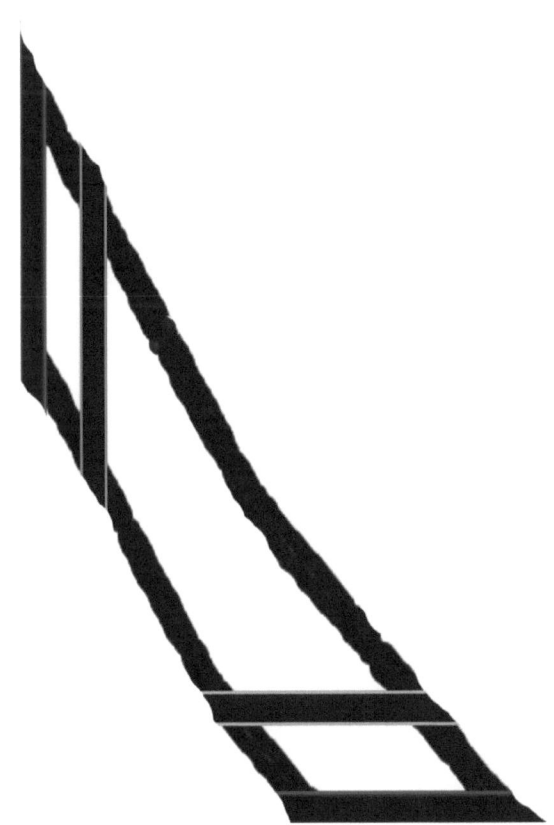

Page 4
Skirt

Page 6
Skirt

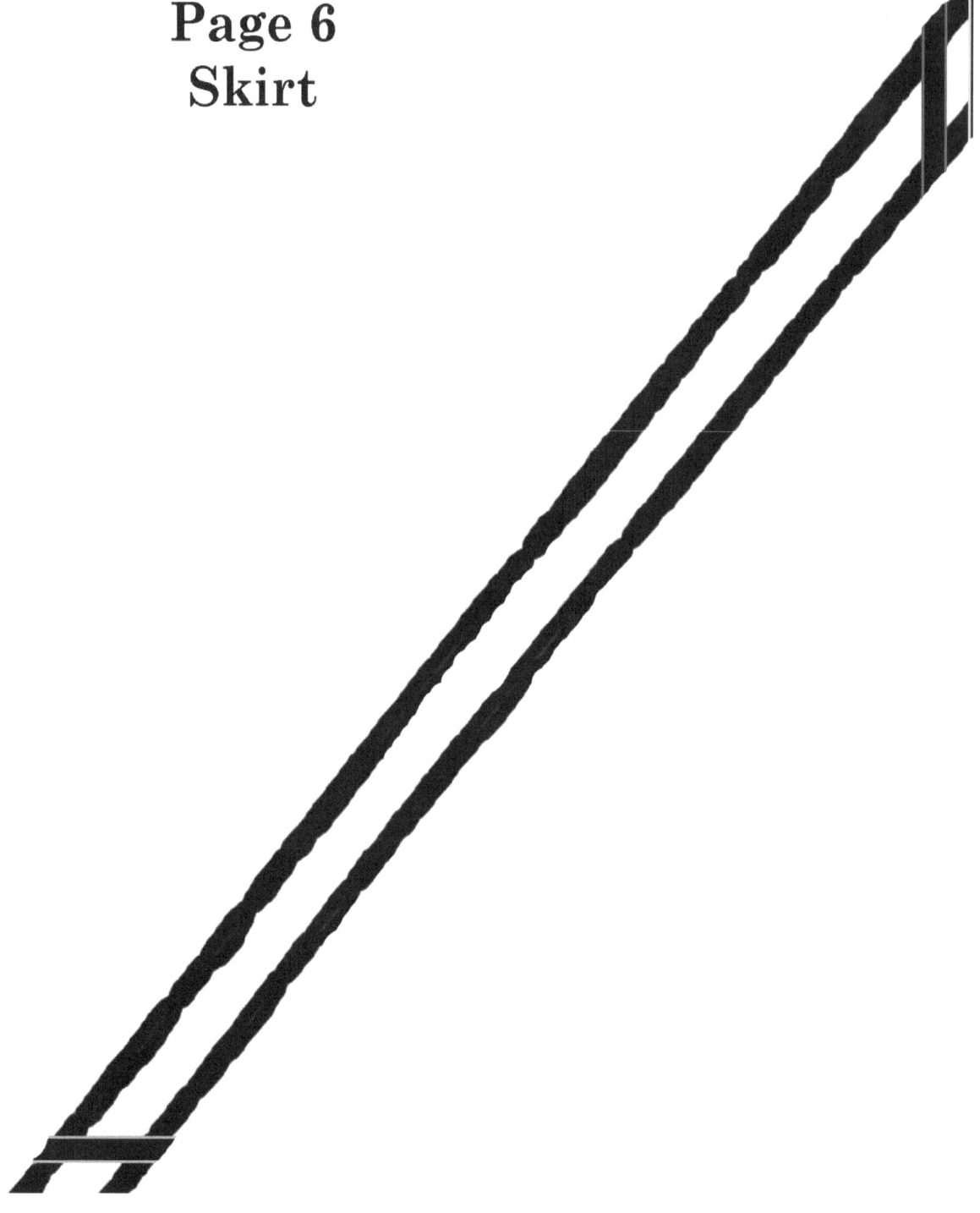

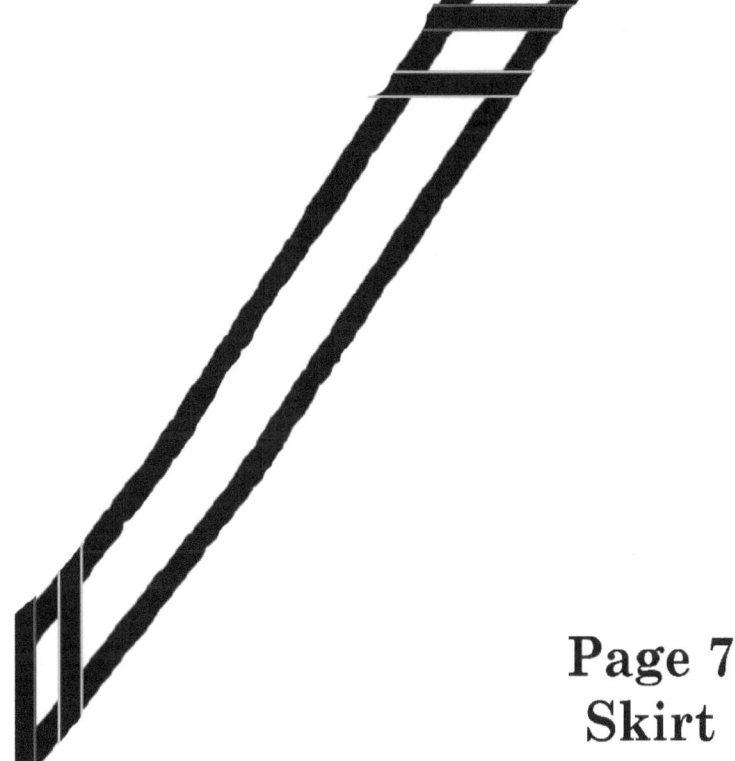

Page 7
Skirt

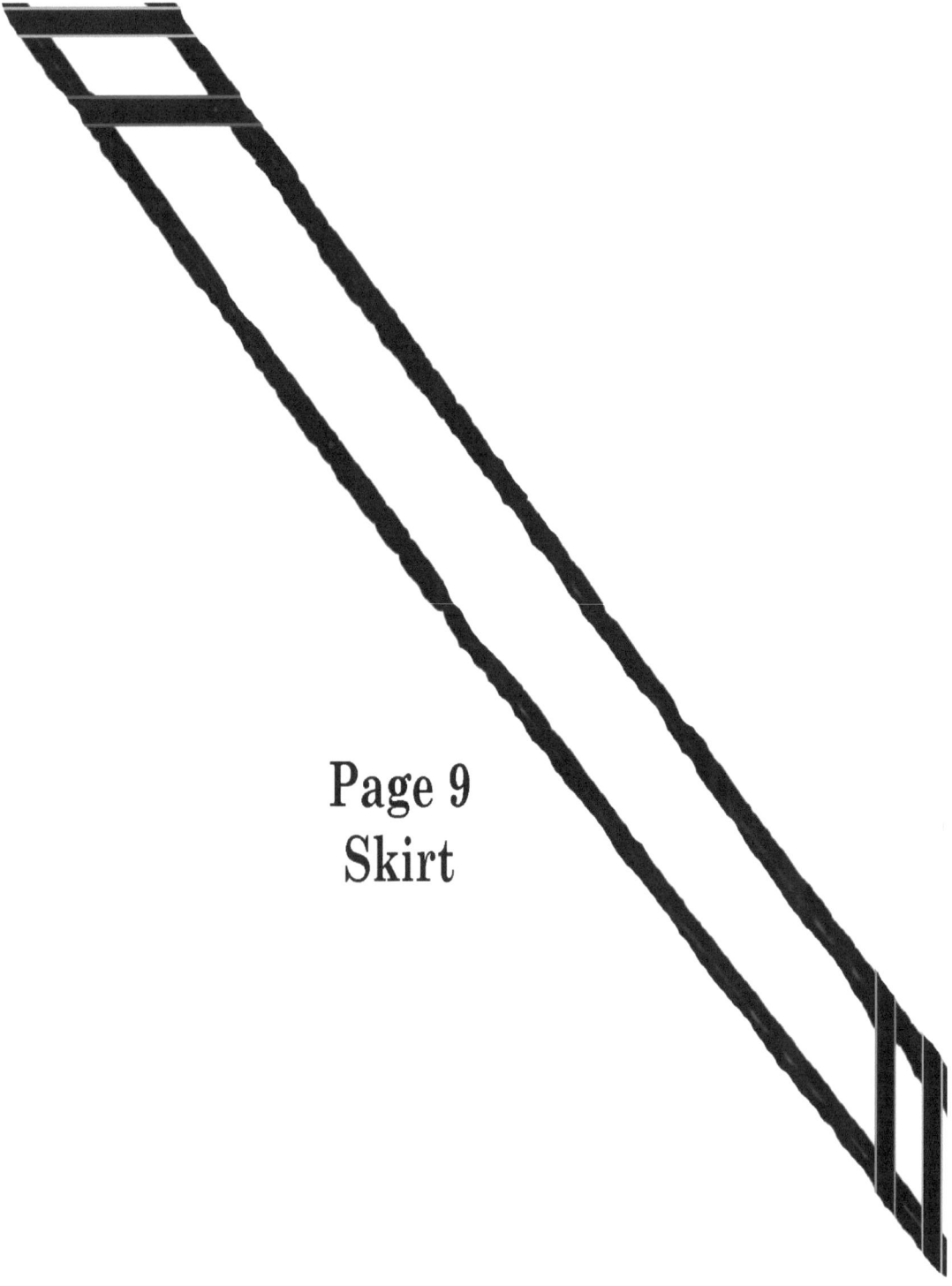

Page 9
Skirt

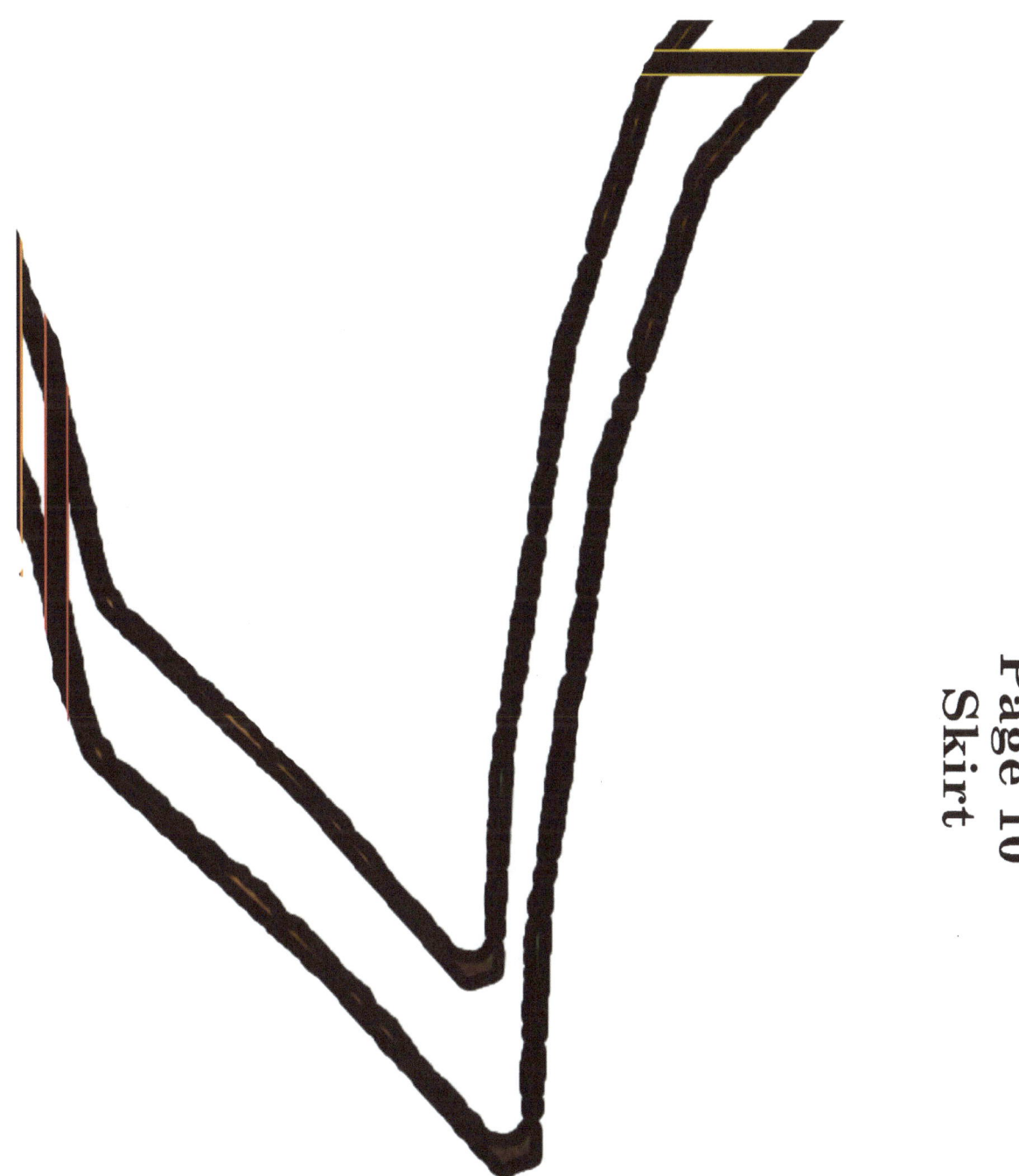

Page 10
Skirt

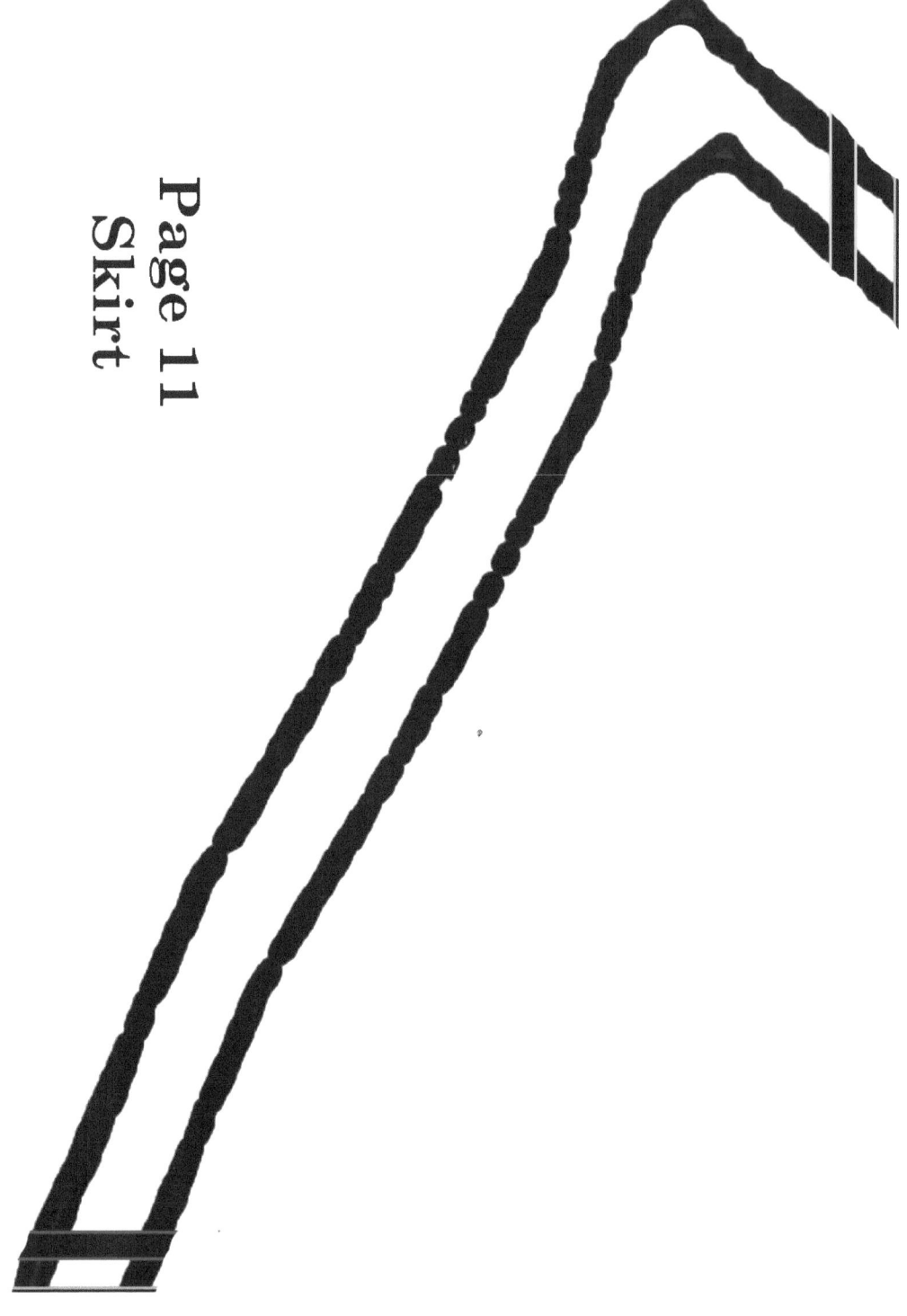

Page 11
Skirt

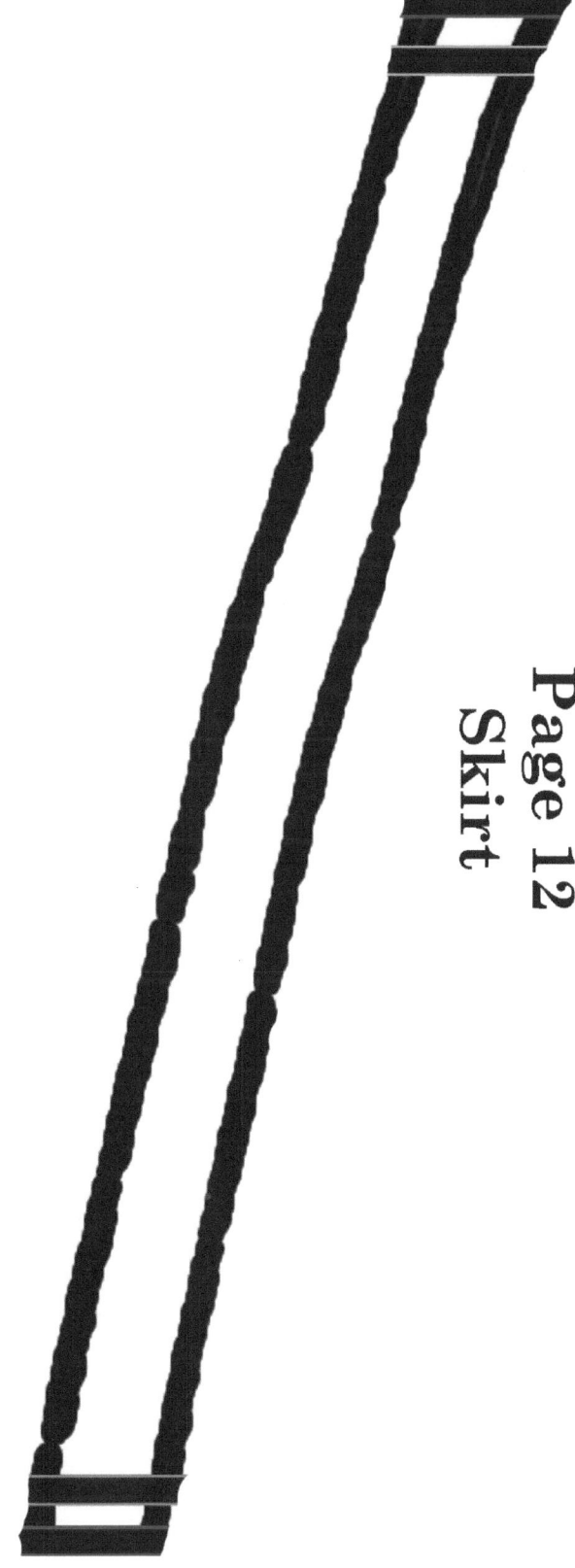

**Page 12
Skirt**

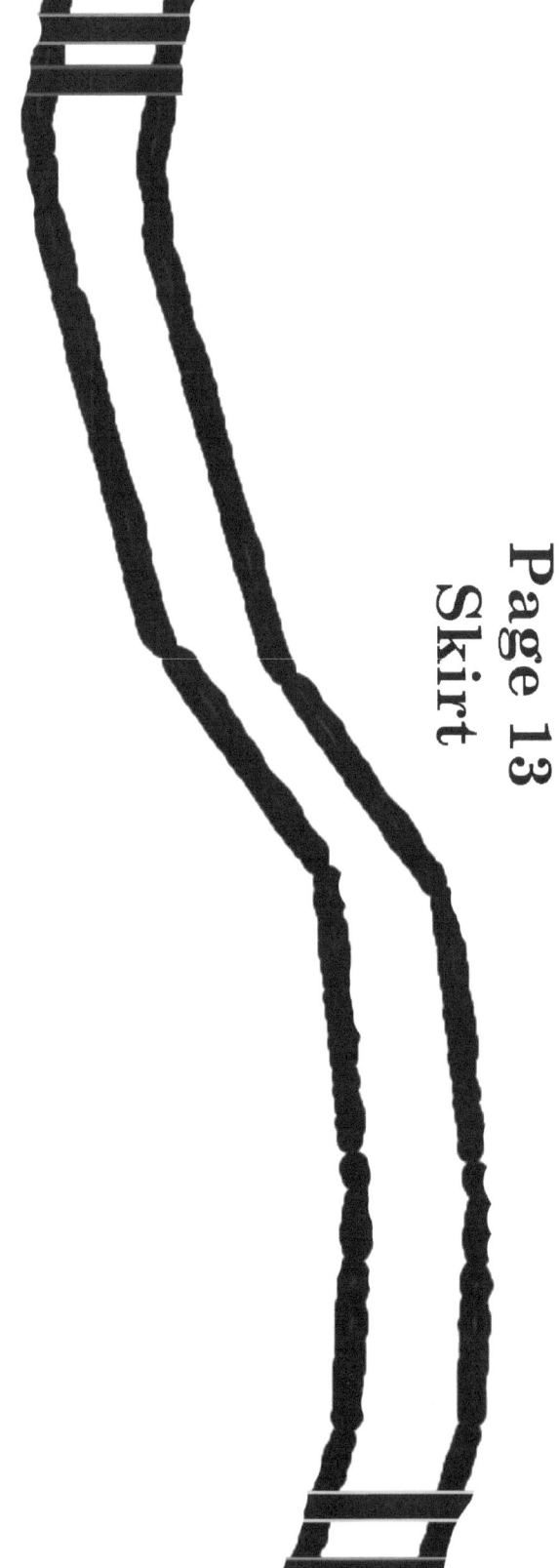

Page 13
Skirt

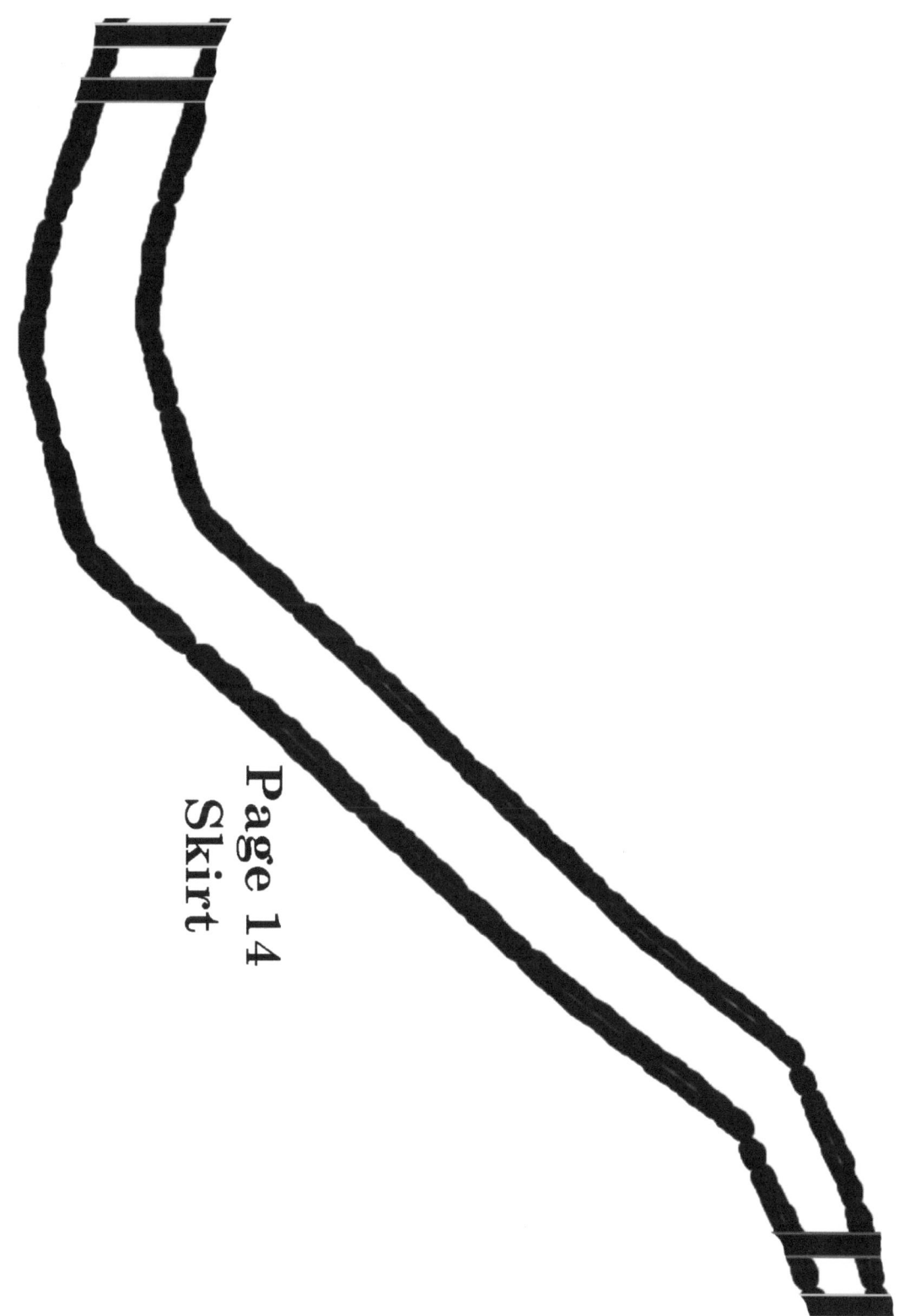

**Page 14
Skirt**

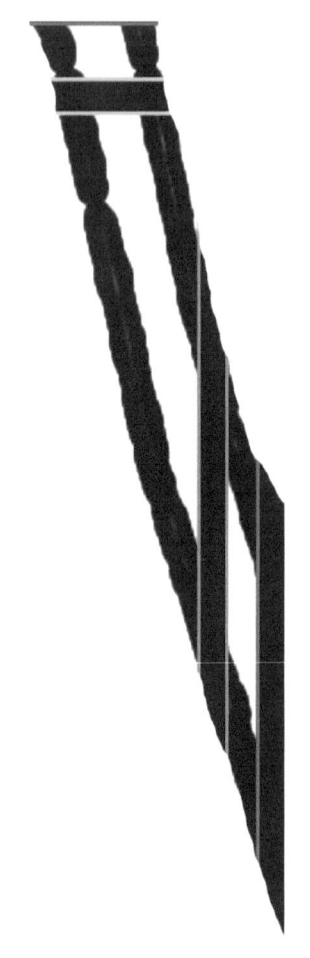

Page 15
Skirt

Hair Pattern

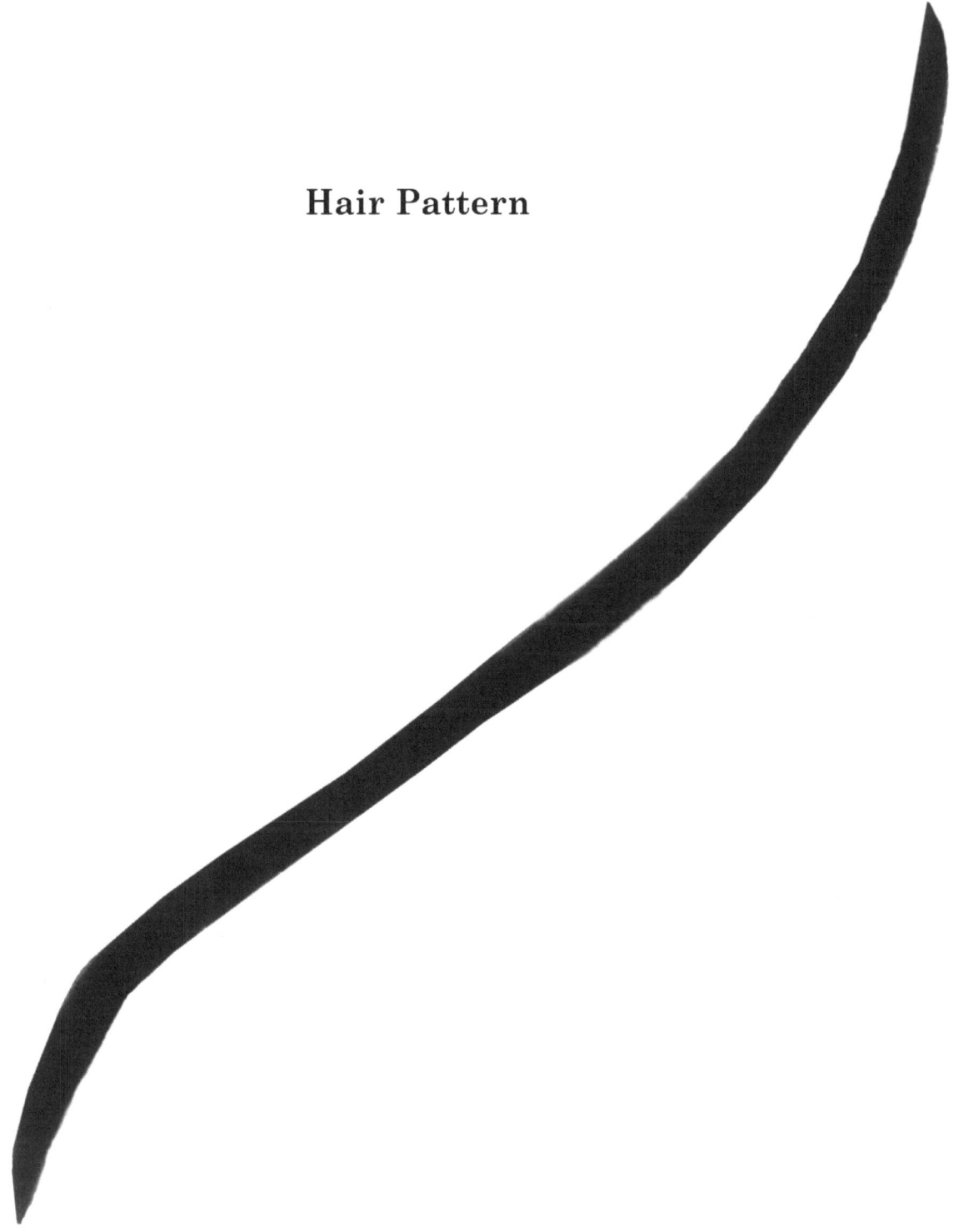

Hair Pattern

**Attach to Page Two to create the length.
Trim and adjust as needed in placement.**

Page One

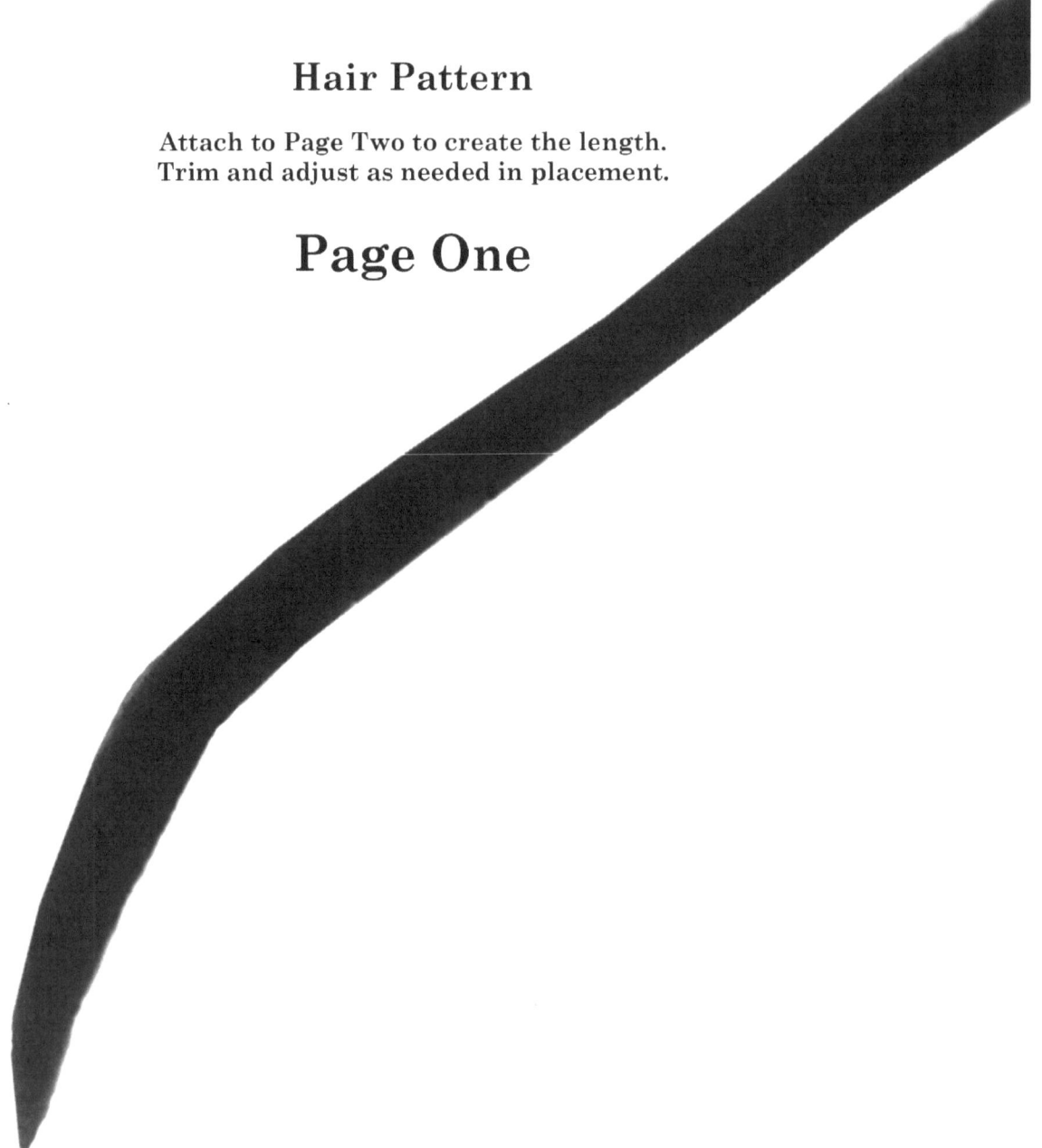

Hair Pattern

**Attach to Page One to create the length.
Trim and adjust as needed in placement.**

Page Two

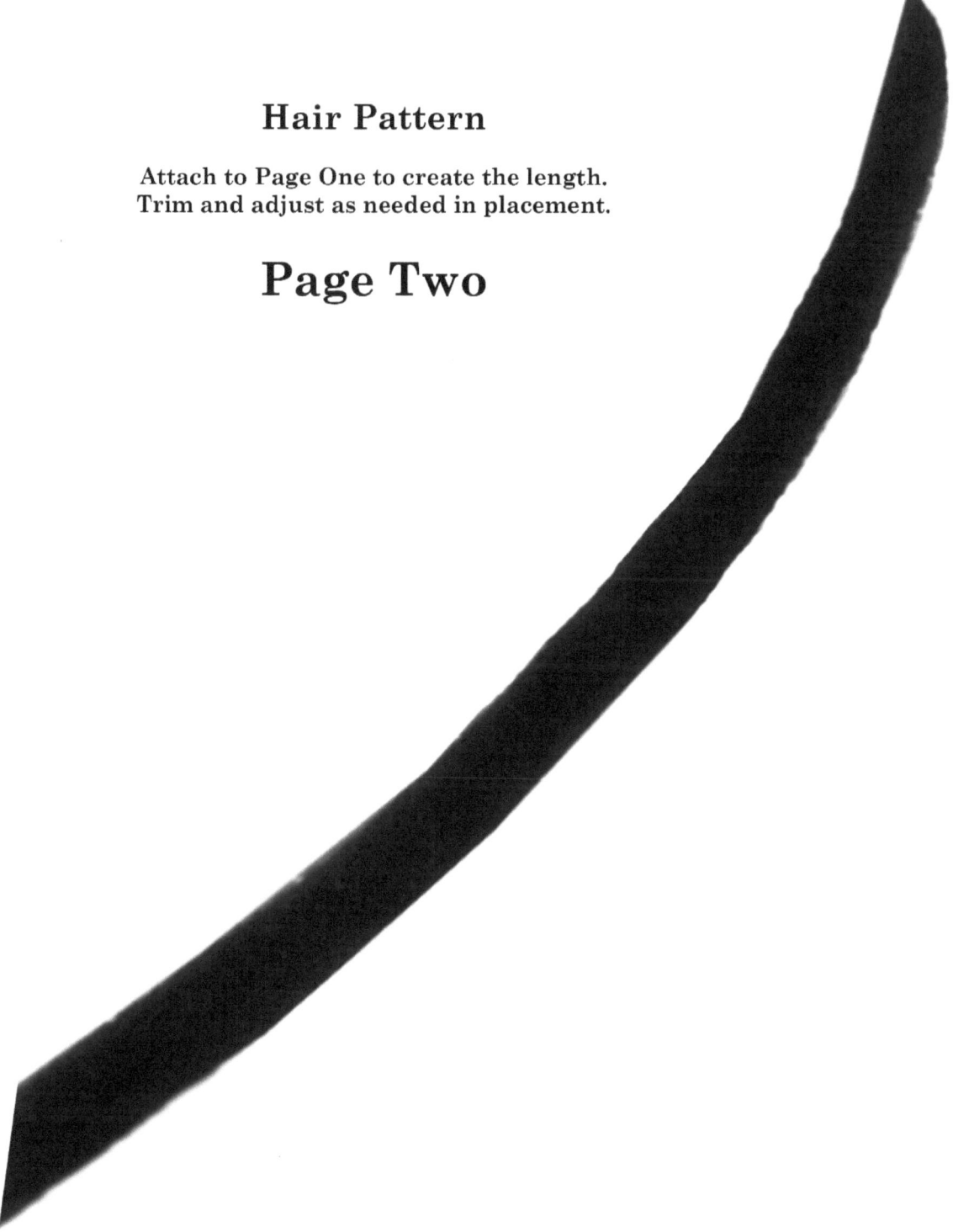

ABOUT THE AUTHOR

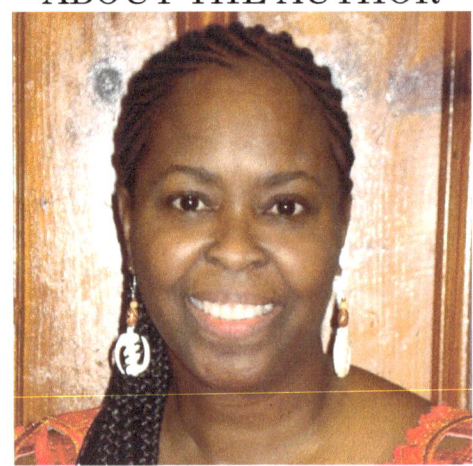

Aisha Lumumba is a well known artist residing in Atlanta, Georgia USA. She was born in a rural suburb of Atlanta, known as McDonough, Georgia. She loves writing and quilting, which led her to write stories and books about quilting. Ms. Lumumba started writing in Elementary School and continues to the present day. She has more than 30 years of quilting experience, not only for practical uses, but as a form of artistic expression.

Ms. Lumumba is very prolific as a quilter and fiber artist. She is a member of the Brown Sugar Stitchers Quilt Guild, Black Art in America and African Americans for the Arts. Her quilts are now a part of the collections of Ambassador Andrew Young, Mrs. Valerie Jackson, Dr. Stephanie Jolly, Ms. Brenda Banks, Ms. Woodie Persons, The Atrium on Sweet Auburn, President & Mrs. Barack Obama and many others.

www.ingramcontent.com/pod-product-compliance
Lightning Source LLC
Chambersburg PA
CBHW040745200526
45159CB00023B/1728